Reading Bridge™
8th grade

Written by:

Leland Graham
and
Darriel Ledbetter

Project Directors: Michele D. Van Leeuwen
Scott G. Van Leeuwen

Creative & Marketing Director: George Starks

Product Development & Design Director: Dante J. Orazzi

Reading Bridge™
8th Grade

All rights reserved.
Copyright ©1999 Rainbow Bridge Publishing

Permission to Reproduce

Copyright ©1999 by Rainbow Bridge Publishing, Salt Lake City, Utah. Rainbow Bridge Publishing grants the right to the individual purchaser to reproduce the student activity materials in this book for noncommercial, individual, or classroom use only. Reproduction for an entire school or school system is strictly prohibited. No part of this publication may be reproduced for storage in a retrieval system, or transmitted in any form or by any means, electronic, mechanical, recording, or otherwise.

For more information write or call:
Rainbow Bridge Publishing
332 West Martin Lane
Salt Lake City, UT 84107
801-268-8887
www.rainbowbridgepub.com

Original Cover Art:
Joe Flores

Copy Editors and/or Proofreaders:
Debbie Armstrong, Angela Erickson, Dante Orazzi, George Starks, Dave Thompson, Carol VanLeeuwen, Lesile Vaughntrap, Kirsten Wille, Dixon

Graphic Design, Illustration and Layout:
Thomas Dyches, Dante Orazzi and Jeffrey Whitehead

Contributing writers:
Marie Ann Bauer, Angela Erickson, Linda Van Loh, Dante Orazzi, George Starks

The authors would like to gratefully acknowledge the assistance and suggestions
of the following persons:
Debbie Armstrong, William Baker, Becky Lee, Beverly Moody, Dan Payne, and John Spilane

Printed by Press America in the U.S.A.

Printing History:
First Printing 1999
Second Printing 2000

ISBN: 1-887923-15-2

Printed in the United States of America
10 9 8 7 6 5 4 3 2 1

Table of Contents

Introduction	4
Bananas	8
The Monster	10
Will Smith	12
Where's Joey?	14
Ode to a Dying World	18
Autumn Sun	18
Baghdad	20
Graduation!	22
Chapters	25
The Bald Eagle	28
The Accident	30
The Rose: An Essay	32
Coming Home	34
End of the Night	37
Is There Really an Atlantis?	38
The Key	40
The Race of a Lifetime	42
A Southern Christmas: An Essay	46
Mad King Prey	48
My Eighth Grade English Journal	51
The Allure of South Dakota	53
Marley the Magician	56
Gentle Owners	58
Moonlit Night	60
Blue	60
'Lories	62
Lonely: An Essay	65
Good-bye Tomorrow	67
The Coldest Place on Earth	70
Colors of Christmas	72
Miracle Drugs	74
In My Dreams	76
Ice Cream Memories	77
Baby's First Thoughts	80
Mariah Carey	82
The Growing Process	84
Tulips	84
Gypsies	86
Hillary Rodham Clinton	88
Charleston	90
Writing Challenge	92
Capitalization & Grammar Guide	93
Grammar Guide	94
Check Yourself	95

Prepares Students For Standardized Achievement Tests

Introduction

The **Reading Bridge** series is designed to improve and motivate students' reading. This book has been developed to provide eighth grade students practical skill-based exercises in the areas of inferences, main ideas, cause and effect, fact and opinion, and figurative language. The purpose of this book is to familiarize students with the kinds of reading tasks they will encounter on a daily basis. Furthermore, reading will enrich and facilitate their lives as young adults in an ever-changing world that has information readily available, but only if they learn to take advantage of and appreciate reading.

The stories, poems, and essays, in this collection are each accompanied by exercises that address reading skills. Each story, poem or essay has been written so that students at the eighth grade level can read it successfully. The carefully thought-out questions will help your students learn to think, inquire, create, imagine, respond and in some instances, do research to learn more about a specific topic.

The **Capitalization and Grammar Guide** found at the back of the book has been included to help students better understand common grammar found in day-to-day reading.

Reading Bridge adapts to any teaching situation whether at home or in the classroom. It can be used in many different ways. For instance:

- ✔ **For at home practice:** this series is ideal to supplement or extend school work and home school reading programs.

- ✔ **For the entire class:** this series can be used for intensive reinforcement of reading skills or to simply supplement a basal reading program.

- ✔ **For reading groups:** this series will provide skills practice at appropriate levels, and the reading exercises become progressively more challenging.

- ✔ **For individual use:** this series will help build a completely individualized program.

Use Your Dictionary!!!

The English language is made up of thousands and thousands and thousands of words; so many words that it would be impossible for you to know what every single one of these words means! But wait! Just because you come across a word in this book, or somewhere else, that may be unfamiliar to you, does not mean that you should ignore it or give up on learning its meaning.

Instead, use a dictionary to learn the meaning of the word you don't know. You'll get better scores on the exercises in this book. More importantly, you'll expand your knowledge base and become a better communicator because you'll be able to both express yourself and understand other people more clearly!

Dic • tion • ar • y, n. **1.** a book of alphabetically listed words in a language, with definitions, pronunciations, and other information about the words

8th Grade Reading List

Aiken, Joan
Wolves of Willoughby Chase, The

Armstrong, William
Sounder

Avi
Nothing But the Truth

Babbitt, Natalie
Search for Delicious, The

Barron, T.A.
Ancient One, The

Birdseye, Tom
Tucker

Bond, Nancy
String in the Harp, A

Burch, Robert
Queenie Peavy

Burnett, Frances
Little Princess, A
Secret Garden, The

Burnford, Shelia
Incredible Journey, The

Calvert, Patricia
Snowbird, The

Choi, Sook Nyul
Year of Impossible Goodbyes

Cleaver, Vera
Where the Lilies Bloom

Cooper, Susan
Grey King, The
Over Sea, Under Stone

Corcoran, Barbara
Sky is Falling, The

Crew, Linda
Children of the River

Cushman, Karen
Catherine, Called Birdy

Dahl, Roald
James and the Giant Peach

Daugherty, James
Daniel Boone

DeAngeli, Maguerite
Door in the Wall, The

DeSaint-Exupery, A.
Little Prince, The

DeTrevino, Elizabeth
I, Juan de Pareja

DuBois, William
Twenty-One Balloons, The

Eckert, Allan W.
Incident at Hawk's Hill

Edwards, Julie
Last of the Really Great Whangdoodles

Enright, Elizabeth
Gone-Away Lake

Estes, Eleanor
Hundred Dresses, The

Field, Rachel
Hitty, Her First Hundred Years

Fitzgerald, John D.
Great Brain at the Academy, The

Forbes, Esther
Johnny Tremain

Fox, Paula
Slave Dancer, The

Freedman, Russell
Wright Brothers . . . Airplane, The

Gannett, Ruth S.
My Father's Dragon

Gray, Elizabeth J.
Adam of the Road

Guy, Rosa
Music of Summer, The

Hahn, Mary Downing
Spanish Kidnapping Disaster, The

Heide, Florence
Banana Twist

Holm, Anne
North to Freedom

Hudson, Jan
Sweetgrass

Hunt, Irene
Across Five Aprils
Up a Road Slowly

James, Will
Smoky the Cow Horse

Juster, Norton
Phantom Tollbooth, The

Keith, Harold
Rifles for Watie

Kelly, Eric P.
Trumpeter of Krakow, The

Kendall, Carol
Gammage Cup, The

Krumgold, Joseph
And Now Miguel

L'Engle, Madeleine
Ring of Endless Light, A

Langton, Jane
Fledgling, The

8th Grade Reading List

Lawson, Robert
Ben and Me
Rabbit Hill

LeGuin, Ursula K.
Tombs of Atuan, The

Lewis, Elizabeth
Young Fu of the Upper Yangtze

Lindbergh, Anne
Travel Far, Pay No Fare

Lindgren, Astrid
Pippi Longstocking

Lofting, Hugh
Voyages of Doctor Dolittle, The

London, Jack
Call of the Wild, The
White Fang

Lowry, Lois
Anastasia at Your Service
Taking Care of Terrific

Lyons, Mary E.
Letters from a Slave Girl

McKinley, Robin
Blue Sword, The
Hero and the Crown, The

Meigs, Cornelia
Willow Whistle, The

Merrill, Jean
Pushcart War, The

Montgomery, L.M.
Anne of Green Gables

Naidoo, Beverly
Chain of Fire

Nhuong, Huynh Quan
Land I Lost, The

North, Sterling
Rascal

Paterson, Katherine
Bridge to Terabithia
Jacob I Have Loved

Pullman, Philip
Detective Stories

Reeder, Carolyn
Foster's War

Richter, Conrad
Light in the Forest, The

Roberts, Willo D.
Baby-Sitting is a Dangerous Job

Rottman, S.L.
Rough Waters

Ruckman, Ivy
Night of the Twisters

Seredy, Kate
White Stag, The

Sewell, Anna
Black Beauty

Sidney, Margaret
Five Little Peppers and How They Grew

Smith, Roland
Sasquatch

Snyder, Zilpha K.
Headless Cupid, The
Witches of Worm, The

Stevermer, Caroline
River Rats

Taylor, Mildred
Let the Circle Be Unbroken
Roll of Thunder, Hear My Cry

Taylor, Theodore
Cay, The

Temple, Frances
Taste of Salt

Thesman, Jean
When the Road Ends

Travers, P.L.
Mary Poppins

Van Leeuwen, Jean
Great Summer Camp Catastrophe

Walsh, Jill Paton
Green Book, The

Yep, Laurence
Dragonwings

Zindel, Paul
Pigman and Me, The
Reef of Death

Incentive Contract

In • cen'tive, n. 1. Something that urges a person on. 2. Enticing. 3. Encouraging 4. That which excites to action or moves the mind.

Below, List Your Agreed-Upon Incentive for Each Story Group

Student's Signature   **Parent, Teacher, or Guardian Signature**

_____   _____

Place a ✓ after each story & exercise upon completion

Page	Story & Exercise Title		Page	Story & Exercise Title	
8	Bananas		53	The Allure of South Dakota	
10	The Monster		56	Marley the Magician	
12	Will Smith		58	Gentle Owners	
14	Where's Joey?		60	Moonlit Night	
18	Ode to a Dying World		60	Blue	
18	Autumn Sun		62	'Lories	
20	Baghdad		65	Lonely: An Essay	
22	Graduation!		67	Good-bye Tomorrow	
25	Chapters		70	The Coldest Place on Earth	
28	The Bald Eagle		72	Colors of Christmas	
My Incentive Is				**My Incentive Is**	

Page	Story & Exercise Title		Page	Story & Exercise Title	
30	The Accident		74	Miracle Drugs	
32	The Rose: An Essay		76	In My Dreams	
34	Coming Home		77	Ice Cream Memories	
37	End of the Night		80	Baby's First Thoughts	
38	Is There Really an Atlantis?		82	Mariah Carey	
40	The Key		84	The Growing Process	
42	The Race of a Lifetime		84	Tulips	
46	A Southern Christmas: An Essay		86	Gypsies	
48	Mad King Prey		88	Hillary Rodham Clinton	
51	My Eighth Grade English Journal		90	Charleston	
My Incentive Is				**My Incentive Is**	

Bananas

Well, here I am, eighteen and on my own, in New York City, "the city of dreams," or so they say. Hallelujah! Oh, sure, my parents begged me not to leave home at first, but there's no way I was going to enter a religious convent!

"Molly, you're going to be a nun!" My Mom **proclaimed.**

"You're going to make us proud," Dad agreed.

In the end, my parents supported me in doing what I had to do to follow my dreams. I came to New York so I could be a star! I'm going straight to the top! I'm not quite sure how I'm going to be famous, or exactly where in this huge city I need to start to accomplish my goal. But I'm working on figuring it out. It seems that I will need more than a pretty face and a good smile, though, according to the bus driver, I at least have these!

Buses are not the best type of transportation, because you can waste a lot of time waiting around for the right bus. However, I cannot afford to take cabs that much. Even the hotel I am staying in is cheap. It's not the flashing neon sign that lights up my room, or the bars on the windows which make me feel like I am in a jail cell. I am nervous because I read somewhere that if the hotel where you are staying makes you leave a deposit for linen and towels and makes you pay for soap, it just isn't a four-star place. Maybe I am just being **paranoid.** Oh well, at least it has a bed, because I really need a good night's sleep. Tomorrow, I have an important interview, and I definitely do not want circles under my eyes.

Two days ago, I splurged and took a cab. It was one of the scariest experiences of my life. I had to tell the driver that if he couldn't make up his mind whether to floor it or brake it, that I would just drive the car myself! In all the commotion, however, the cab driver did manage to ask me the usual questions like: where I was from, how long was I staying, and why was I here. When he learned that I was planning to be famous, he told me about a rehearsal for a banana commercial. I immediately realized that this could be my big opportunity to be discovered!

The rehearsal requires me to wear a banana suit. Isn't that great? This is my big chance, and I don't plan to blow it. I do not intend to be some "wannabe," actress waitressing all her life. If so, I might as well give up now and go home.

Of course, that's not going to happen, because yesterday I purchased the brightest pair of yellow tights I could find. When I put them on, I was the most beautiful banana that ever walked through a department store. Even the lady trying on clothes next to me thought so because she looked at me, laughed and said, "Young lady, it looks like your legs are two giant bananas in those tights."

I thanked her for her input and made my purchase. Then I went to the supermarket and bought some banana flavoring to dab behind my ears. I even found a pin that reads, "Kiss me, I eat a bananas." Even if I don't get the part for my talent as a banana, I should get it for my enthusiasm!

READING CHALLENGE

After reading "Bananas," answer the following questions.

1. When Molly arrived in New York City, she was
   - ○ A. seventeen.
   - ● B. eighteen.
   - ○ C. nineteen.
   - ○ D. twenty.

2. A <u>paranoid</u> person is someone who is
   - ○ A. angry.
   - ○ B. jealous.
   - ● C. suspicious.
   - ○ D. calm.

3. Why is Molly in New York City?
   - ● A. to become famous
   - ○ B. to work in a four-star hotel
   - ○ C. to be a waitress
   - ○ D. to drive a yellow taxi

4. Who advised Molly about the job opening for the banana commercial?
   - ○ A. hotel clerk
   - ○ B. tye-dye manager
   - ○ C. a nun
   - ● D. cab driver

5. The <u>bus driver made a comment about Molly's</u>
   - ○ A. clothes.
   - ● B. pretty face and smile.
   - ○ C. yellow tights.
   - ○ D. parents.

6. Molly's legs looked
   - ○ A. shapely.
   - ● B. like bananas.
   - ○ C. like toothpicks.
   - ○ D. beautiful.

7. "Molly, you're going to be a nun!" my mom <u>proclaimed</u>. Proclaimed means
   - ● A. declared.
   - ○ B. denied.
   - ○ C. wished.
   - ○ D. disclaimed.

8. If Molly does not get the part for her talent, perhaps she will get it for her
   - ○ A. beauty.
   - ● B. enthusiasm.
   - ○ C. politics.
   - ○ D. negativity.

Total Correct _____

The Monster

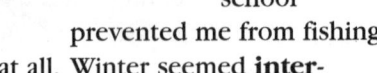

As winter slowly merges into spring, the anticipation of fishing with my dad in our favorite pond grows. The pond is surrounded by large oak trees and tall grass, which help provide a natural habitat for all kinds of fish. The grass has been bitten by spring frost that forms during the cool nights, but the trees are starting to bud as the days become warmer. To reach the pond, my dad and I have to tromp through endless pastures of milkweed, around sinkholes large enough to swallow a horse, and over a slow-running creek that contains small bait fish.

Overgrown shrubbery and towering pine trees hide the fish pond, so not many people fish here. My dad once told me that he caught four fish in 30 minutes at this pond! They weighed three, four, six, and seven pounds! Dad has been fishing here all of his life. He fishes in any kind of weather, even in the rain.

Once, when I was thirteen, my dad and I were out fishing. Suddenly, my line shot straight out from the bank. A huge bass leapt out of the water. That was the biggest bass my dad and I had ever seen! When it jumped out of the water, it spit the plastic worm out of its mouth and escaped. Even though I didn't catch that bass, I vowed I would come back for it! One month later, I attempted to hook him again — no success.

Summer finally arrived, and I still hadn't caught that bass, so I tried fishing in other places to get my mind off of him. One weekend my dad and I fished at Smith Lake in Alabama. The next weekend we drove to Tennessee to fish in a tributary of the Ocoee River. We caught many fish that day, including three that weighed around three, six, and eight pounds. But even though this was great, I still wanted to nail that big old bass!

Late in the summer I still had not caught the **elusive** fish. When school began, we could not fish as much, and for about two months, the weather and school prevented me from fishing at all. Winter seemed **interminable**, and I hardly fished any more. My mind was now preoccupied with hunting, especially since I purchased a new sport rifle. Still, I don't enjoy hunting as much as I do fishing.

When spring arrived, I headed down to our favorite pond to fish for that "monster," bass. After three weeks of fishing, I finally got a strong bite. Thinking it was The Monster, I became excited, but it was only a two-pounder. However, I knew the slippery monster would soon nibble my line! That day I renewed my vow never to give up!

Around mid summer, I felt a familiar tug at my line. I knew it was my monster bass! Relaxed and cool, not rushing or too anxious, I carefully reeled in my line. It took about 15 minutes, and although it did not fight as much as I thought it would, my arms were sore and numb by the time I pulled him squirming out of the water. I was victorious! The "monster," was mine!

I immediately weighed the bass on a scale that I carried in my tackle box. He topped the scale at twelve pounds and seven ounces, but I could tell by the spots along his spine, and his coloring, that he was very old. After two years of trying to catch him, I felt excited, yet strangely depressed. I was especially proud that I had caught him. I felt this was the most memorable moment of my life, but I knew this exceptional creature belonged in his watery habitat, not on my bedroom wall. I released the old "monster," back into the water. Fishing for him, not making the catch, had been the adventure.

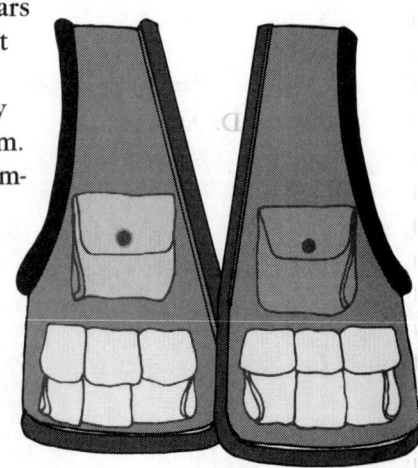

READING CHALLENGE

After reading "The Monster," answer the following questions.

1. The story is mainly about
   A. the adventure, not winning or losing.
   B. enjoying hunting more than fishing.
   C. not respecting natural habitats.
   D. responsibilities in school.

2. <u>Elusive</u> means
   A. friendly.
   B. evasive.
   C. outgoing.
   D. gregarious.

3. During which season does the narrator catch the "monster?"
   A. winter
   B. spring
   C. fall
   D. summer

4. How long did it take to catch the "monster?"
   A. two months
   B. two years
   C. four months
   D. three years

5. How large are the sinkholes that are found on the way to the pond?
   A. as large as a big fish
   B. as large as a man
   C. as large as a horse
   D. as large as a towering pine tree

6. How long is winter if it is <u>interminable</u>?
   A. endless
   B. limited
   C. short
   D. only 2 months

7. Smith Lake is located in
   A. Tennessee.
   B. Alabama.
   C. California.
   D. Georgia.

8. The narrator was more preoccupied with hunting, than fishing, because
   A. he didn't get a new rod.
   B. the pond was frozen.
   C. he was tired of fishing.
   D. he purchased a new sport rifle.

Remember, if you don't know what a word means, look it up in a dictionary! You'll do better in the exercises!

Total Correct _____   11

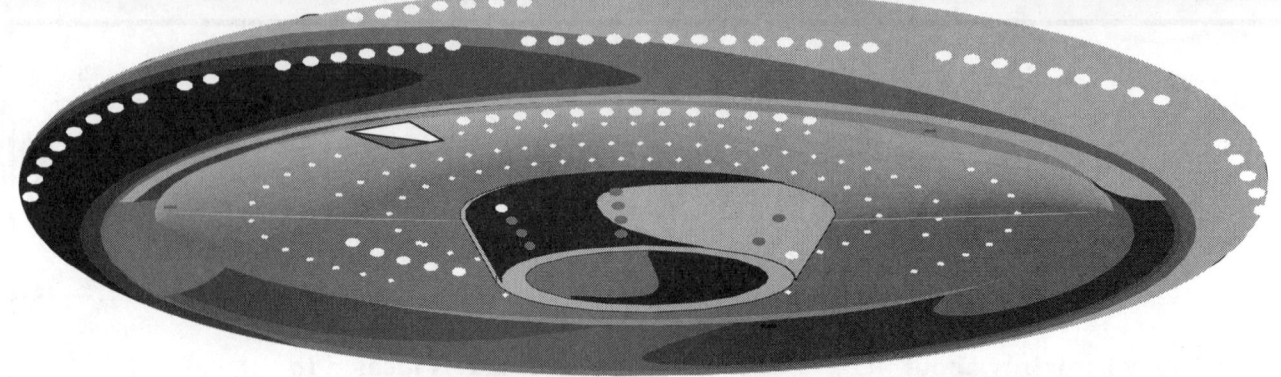

WILL SMITH

Will Smith has starred in several movies, had his own television show, and has, so far, recorded four CD's. His career has taken him from a musical recording artist to a television and movie star. The hit movie *Independence Day*, in which Will co-starred, made ninety-six million dollars in the first days of its release. Two of his four CD's went platinum. Will is a **dynamic** entertainer in any **medium**.

Will Smith, known to many as "The Fresh Prince," is the son of Will and Caroline Smith. The second of four children, he was born and raised in a middle-class neighborhood in west Philadelphia.

When he was sixteen years old, Will had the opportunity to meet Jeff Townes, who was the deejay at a friend's party. They became friends and started performing at clubs under the name "DJ Jazzy Jeff and the Fresh Prince." In 1986, they made their first CD, *Rock the House*, which sold over 600,000 copies. Their 1988 single, "Parents Just Don't Understand," won a Grammy Award for Best Rap Performance, the first award ever given in that category.

In 1989, Will met Benny Medina. Benny wanted to produce a TV show based on Will's life. Will loved the idea, and they invited Quincy Jones to be the Executive Producer. In 1990, Quincy Jones invited NBC executives to his house to view Will's audition for the part. The executives were **ecstatic** and the show, *The Fresh Prince of Bel Air*, was born.

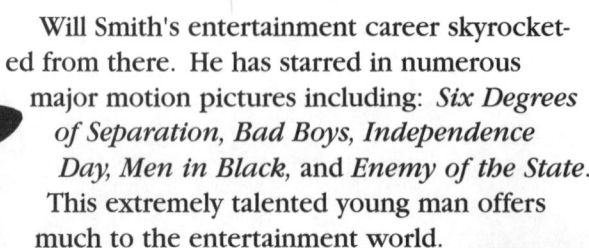

Will Smith's entertainment career skyrocketed from there. He has starred in numerous major motion pictures including: *Six Degrees of Separation, Bad Boys, Independence Day, Men in Black,* and *Enemy of the State*. This extremely talented young man offers much to the entertainment world.

Name ....

READING CHALLENGE

After reading "Will Smith," answer the following questions.

1. What does the word <u>ecstatic</u> mean?

2. A nickname for Will Smith, as well as part of a name for a TV show, is ___*Fresh Prince*___.

3. DJ Jazzy Jeff and The Fresh Prince's first CD that sold over 600,000 copies was called ___*Rock the house*___.

4. Who was the Executive Producer, along with NBC executives, of the show "The Fresh Prince of Bel Air"? *Quincy Jones*

5. Pertaining to or characterized by energy is the meaning of the word ___*dynamic*___.

6. List the five major motion pictures mentioned in this article.
Six degrees of separation
Independence day
Men in Black
Enemy of the state

7. Will Smith's talent has taken him into what three categories?
music, movies, TV show

8. In which hit movie did Will Smith co-star that made ninety-six million dollars in the first days of its release? *Independence day*

9. <u>Means</u> and <u>instrument</u> are definitions for which word? *medium*

10. In 1988, the single ___*Parents just don't understand*___ won a Grammy for Best Rap Performance, the first award ever given in that category.

Reading to Write

11. In a well-developed paragraph, discuss or describe one of your role models who has influenced your life. Include why the person has had a major impact on your life and how you have become a better person as a result of knowing this person.

Total Correct _____   13

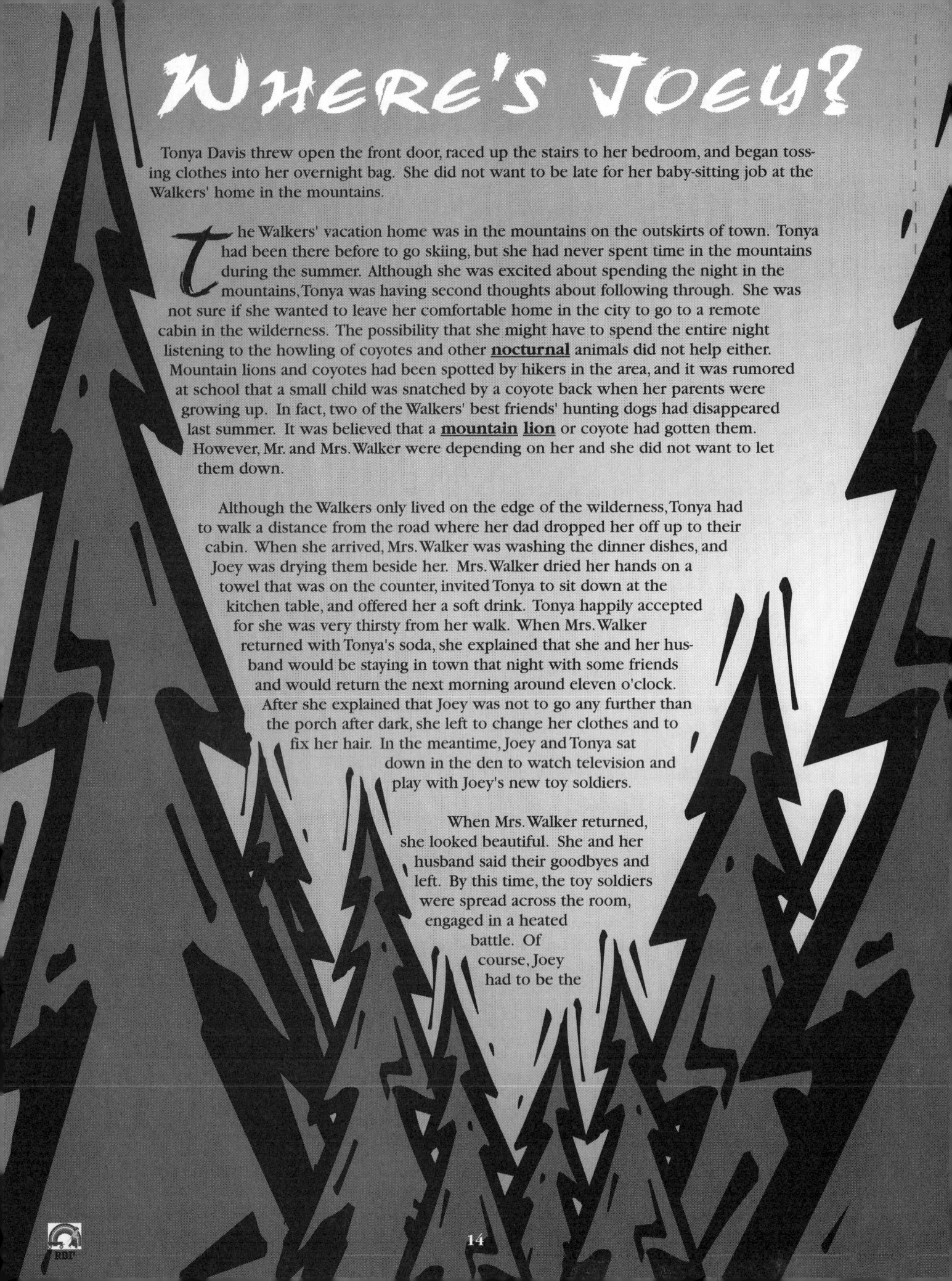

Where's Joey?

Tonya Davis threw open the front door, raced up the stairs to her bedroom, and began tossing clothes into her overnight bag. She did not want to be late for her baby-sitting job at the Walkers' home in the mountains.

The Walkers' vacation home was in the mountains on the outskirts of town. Tonya had been there before to go skiing, but she had never spent time in the mountains during the summer. Although she was excited about spending the night in the mountains, Tonya was having second thoughts about following through. She was not sure if she wanted to leave her comfortable home in the city to go to a remote cabin in the wilderness. The possibility that she might have to spend the entire night listening to the howling of coyotes and other **nocturnal** animals did not help either. Mountain lions and coyotes had been spotted by hikers in the area, and it was rumored at school that a small child was snatched by a coyote back when her parents were growing up. In fact, two of the Walkers' best friends' hunting dogs had disappeared last summer. It was believed that a **mountain lion** or coyote had gotten them. However, Mr. and Mrs. Walker were depending on her and she did not want to let them down.

Although the Walkers only lived on the edge of the wilderness, Tonya had to walk a distance from the road where her dad dropped her off up to their cabin. When she arrived, Mrs. Walker was washing the dinner dishes, and Joey was drying them beside her. Mrs. Walker dried her hands on a towel that was on the counter, invited Tonya to sit down at the kitchen table, and offered her a soft drink. Tonya happily accepted for she was very thirsty from her walk. When Mrs. Walker returned with Tonya's soda, she explained that she and her husband would be staying in town that night with some friends and would return the next morning around eleven o'clock. After she explained that Joey was not to go any further than the porch after dark, she left to change her clothes and to fix her hair. In the meantime, Joey and Tonya sat down in the den to watch television and play with Joey's new toy soldiers.

When Mrs. Walker returned, she looked beautiful. She and her husband said their goodbyes and left. By this time, the toy soldiers were spread across the room, engaged in a heated battle. Of course, Joey had to be the

14

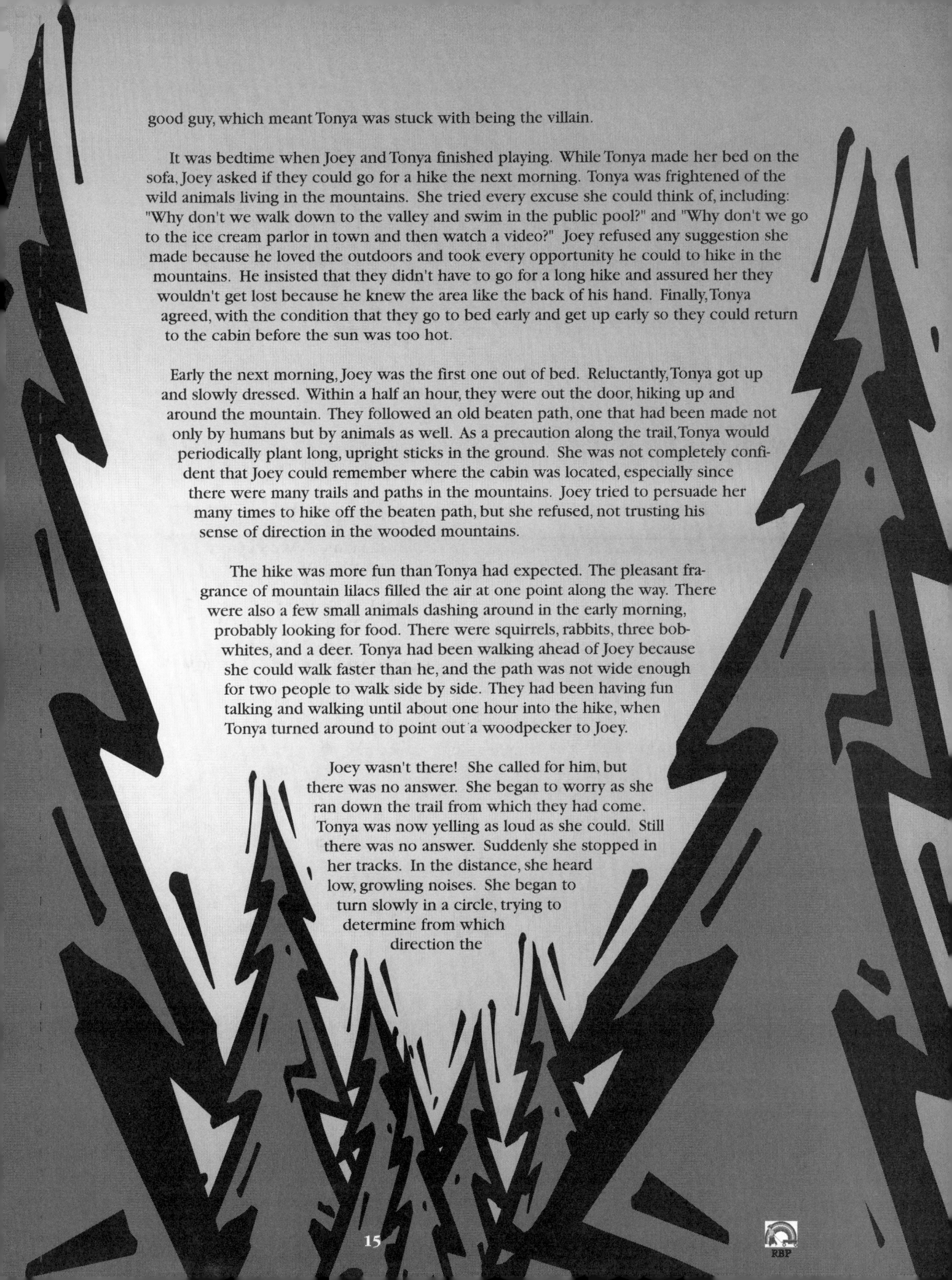

good guy, which meant Tonya was stuck with being the villain.

It was bedtime when Joey and Tonya finished playing. While Tonya made her bed on the sofa, Joey asked if they could go for a hike the next morning. Tonya was frightened of the wild animals living in the mountains. She tried every excuse she could think of, including: "Why don't we walk down to the valley and swim in the public pool?" and "Why don't we go to the ice cream parlor in town and then watch a video?" Joey refused any suggestion she made because he loved the outdoors and took every opportunity he could to hike in the mountains. He insisted that they didn't have to go for a long hike and assured her they wouldn't get lost because he knew the area like the back of his hand. Finally, Tonya agreed, with the condition that they go to bed early and get up early so they could return to the cabin before the sun was too hot.

Early the next morning, Joey was the first one out of bed. Reluctantly, Tonya got up and slowly dressed. Within a half an hour, they were out the door, hiking up and around the mountain. They followed an old beaten path, one that had been made not only by humans but by animals as well. As a precaution along the trail, Tonya would periodically plant long, upright sticks in the ground. She was not completely confident that Joey could remember where the cabin was located, especially since there were many trails and paths in the mountains. Joey tried to persuade her many times to hike off the beaten path, but she refused, not trusting his sense of direction in the wooded mountains.

The hike was more fun than Tonya had expected. The pleasant fragrance of mountain lilacs filled the air at one point along the way. There were also a few small animals dashing around in the early morning, probably looking for food. There were squirrels, rabbits, three bobwhites, and a deer. Tonya had been walking ahead of Joey because she could walk faster than he, and the path was not wide enough for two people to walk side by side. They had been having fun talking and walking until about one hour into the hike, when Tonya turned around to point out a woodpecker to Joey.

Joey wasn't there! She called for him, but there was no answer. She began to worry as she ran down the trail from which they had come. Tonya was now yelling as loud as she could. Still there was no answer. Suddenly she stopped in her tracks. In the distance, she heard low, growling noises. She began to turn slowly in a circle, trying to determine from which direction the

15

WHERE'S JOEY? CONTINUED

noises were coming. Tonya could not decide. It seemed the noises came from all around her. The thought of "coyotes," loomed in her mind. She began running back to the cabin.

Safely inside the cabin, Tonya quickly dialed 911 and told the dispatcher her story. The dispatcher told her to remain calm, and that the police were on their way. She then called the Walkers in town.

When the police and the Walkers arrived, Tonya explained what had happened to everyone as they hurried up the trail where she and Joey had been walking. They searched for four hours before they found the first clue. One of Joey's tennis shoes was found on a side trail. Mrs. Walker became hysterical, as everyone began to think the worst!

By five o'clock, the search party had scanned a one-mile radius of the area immediately **adjacent** to the Walkers' cabin. Tonya was blaming herself because she was the "adult," in charge. She really hoped Joey was safe.

About six o'clock, Tonya insisted that some people in the search party return with her to the spot where she first heard the growling noises. After scanning the area once again, Tonya was about to give up when she heard a whimpering noise coming from above. Still thinking of coyotes, neither Tonya nor the policeman with her were eager to discover the whereabouts of the noise. Walking slowly and with **trepidation**, they made their way in the direction of the noise.

Tonya heard someone calling her name. It sounded muffled and smothered, but she immediately recognized Joey's voice. She began yelling and rushing forward, not knowing where to run because he was not visible. Jeff, the policeman, spotted him high up in a tree, trembling and afraid to come down.

After what seemed to be an eternity, Joey was helped down from the tree. He was so afraid! It seemed that Joey had lagged too far behind Tonya and had decided to take another trail. After a few minutes on the new trail, he had decided to climb a tree to see if he could locate Tonya from above. When he got to the top he got scared and could not climb down. Joey had been stuck in the tree all day!

When they found the others, Joey's mom and dad were so happy that they laughed and cried at the same time. Tonya was happy, too. Not only had Joey been found, but she realized that her imagination had gotten the best of her!

READING CHALLENGE

After reading "Where's Joey?," answer the following questions.

1. The story is mainly about
   A. hiking.
   B. baby-sitting.
   C. responsibility and reliability.
   D. living in the mountains.

2. What does the word <u>adjacent</u> mean?
   A. near
   B. distant
   C. apart
   D. hazardous

3. Why did Joey get lost in the mountains?
   A. He spotted a rabbit and ran after it.
   B. He hid behind a tree and lost sight of Tonya.
   C. He deliberately wanted to trick Tonya.
   D. He lagged behind and took a different trail.

4. What is a synonym for <u>mountain lion</u>?
   A. tiger
   B. bear
   C. cougar
   D. leopard

5. Why was Tonya dreading to baby-sit Joey?
   A. Joey often misbehaved.
   B. She was tired of baby-sitting in order to make money.
   C. The Walkers lived in the mountains, away from town.
   D. She wanted to stay home and watch her favorite television program.

6. When Joey was found, where was he?
   A. in a tree
   B. in a cave
   C. in a creek
   D. lying on the ground

7. A <u>nocturnal</u> animal is one that
   A. hunts during the day.
   B. lives in remote mountain regions.
   C. attacks only human beings.
   D. roams or prowls at night.

8. Which happened first?
   A. Mrs. Walker dried her hands on a dish towel.
   B. Two of the Walkers' best friends' hunting dogs had disappeared.
   C. Tonya began tossing clothes into her overnight bag.
   D. Joey was helped down from the tree.

Total Correct _____   17

Ode to a Dying World

Oh, Mother Earth,
 forgive us.
  Our **greed** and ignorance
have spoiled your majestic beauty.

We have drained your soil of its richness,
 tarnished the air with clouds of smog,
  dirtied your water with chemical wastes
   and hurt the **endangered** ones.
 For our own selfish desires,
  we are becoming
 not only your worst nightmare
but our own as well.

Forgive us, Mother Earth.
Use your wonderful healing power
to restore the richness of life.
And revive our exhausted planet.

Autumn Sun

Late in September a new sun comes.
The sun of summer makes its final exit,
igniting the day with less radiating beams
and leaving in haste for its rest,
finishing with bright streaks of violets and brilliant blues.

The autumn sun lingers—clouds are stained a radiant orange
with the concern of the new guardian.
The sky sings with velvet pinks and crimson,
while the warmth desperately surrenders to
console us through the lengthening nights.

Name ....

READING CHALLENGE

After reading both poems, circle the best answer for each question.

1. The poem "Autumn Sun," is mainly about
   A. the October sun.
   B. the heat of summer.
   C. clouds and colors.
   D. the beginning of autumn.

2. What is the meaning of <u>endangered</u>?
   A. plentiful
   B. at risk
   C. dangerous
   D. harmless

3. _____ is being addressed in "Ode to a Dying World."
   A. Mother Earth
   B. mother
   C. executioners
   D. we

4. Having <u>greed</u> is being
   A. rich.
   B. mean.
   C. selfish.
   D. spoiled.

5 . . . . bright streaks of violet and brilliant blues. The repetition of the b's is an example of
   A. simile.
   B. alliteration.
   C. pun.
   D. metaphor.

6. In "Ode to a Dying World," why is the poet asking forgiveness from Mother Earth?
   A. because people are destroying the Earth
   B. because the Earth is destroying people
   C. because the poet has destroyed a flower
   D. because the planet is thriving and doing well

7. To <u>console</u> means
   A. to listen.
   B. to lie down.
   C. to comfort.
   D. to sing.

8. In "Autumn Sun," the expression . . . "the sky sings" . . . is an example of
   A. pun.
   B. personification.
   C. rhyme.
   D. metaphor.

Total Correct_____

BAGHDAD

Baghdad, the largest city and capital of Iraq, is also the capital of Baghdad province. The name, which in Persian means the "God-given," has been the name of the city since the eighth century.

Situated along the banks of the Tigris River in the country's center, Baghdad lies about 25 miles north of the parallel river, the Euphrates. Baghdad is situated in a rich river valley, with an extensive irrigation network and it stands at the junction of many of the great trade routes that have shaped the politics and economics of the Middle East.

During the 1991 Persian Gulf War, Baghdad was the target of massive allied air attacks. The bombing destroyed much of the city's **infrastructure**, including several bridges over the Tigris, and military and government sites. Most city landmarks were spared, and reconstruction after the war was rapid.

Summers in Baghdad are hot, with temperatures ranging from 76° to 122° F. Winters are warm, with an average temperature of 55° F. Baghdad has little precipitation, with only six inches of rain reported annually.

The population, although mostly Arab, also has considerable Persian, Armenian, and Kurdish elements. The major trade of the city is in carpets, hides, wool, gum, and dates. Industries include: distilling, oil refining, food processing, tanning, and metalworking. Baghdad traditionally fills its role as an important center of communication and as an essential trade center for the fertile irrigated areas that surround it.

The present city was founded in 762 A.D. on the west bank by the Abbasid Caliph Al Mansur. From that time on, its commercial **supremacy** in the region was unchallenged. The period of the city's greatest glory was under Caliph Harun Al-Rashid during the eighth and ninth centuries. During that time it was one of the greatest cities of Islam.

Today, Baghdad is the home of the ruler and dictator, Saddam Hussein, who rules with a power that many people feel threatens not only his country but surrounding countries as well.

READING CHALLENGE

After reading "Baghdad," circle the best answer for each question.

1. **Infrastructure** includes which of the following?
    A. vegetable markets
    B. department stores
    C. roads
    D. universities

2. **In 1998, Baghdad was ruled by the dictator**
    A. Saddam Hussein.
    B. Harun Al-Rashid.
    C. Abbasid Caliph Al Mansur.
    D. Euphrates Al-Tigris.

3. **Baghdad was the target of massive allied air attacks during the**
    A. Middle East War.
    B. Persian Gulf War.
    C. The Baghdad War.
    D. Abbasid Caliph War.

4. **In Persian, Baghdad means**
    A. Mansur.
    B. Euphrates.
    C. Caliph.
    D. God-given.

5. **The commercial supremacy in the region has been unchallenged. Another word for supremacy is**
    A. greatness.
    B. trade.
    C. obstacle.
    D. handicap.

6. **Baghdad is situated near what two rivers?**
    A. Tigris and Euphrates
    B. Tigris and Mansur
    C. Euphrates and Mansur
    D. Euphrates and Abbasid

7. **The population of Baghdad is composed of**
    A. Arab, Persian, Armenian, Jew.
    B. Arab, Persian, Armenian, Kurd.
    C. Persian, Kurd, Moslem, Slovak.
    D. Armenian, Arab, Persian, Czech.

8. **Winters in Baghdad are warm, with an average temperature of**
    A. 76° F.
    B. 87° F.
    C. 55° F.
    D. 45° F.

9. **The major trade in Baghdad is in**
    A. carpets, hides, wool, leather.
    B. carpets, hides, wool, jewelry.
    C. carpets, hides, wool, gum, dates.
    D. hides, wool, dates, leather.

Remember, if you don't know what a word means, look it up in a dictionary! You'll do better in the exercises!

Total Correct _____

Graduation!

"Yes!" shouted Juan, as he danced around the football stadium.
"Yes!" shouted Jose, as he threw his cap into the air.
"Yes!" shouted Zac, as he crossed the graduation stage.

The graduation ceremonies were over, and the three boys knew they were headed for the beaches of beautiful Panama City, noted for its white sand and blue water. They had planned this trip throughout their senior year, and today it was about to start.

They left Atlanta on that sultry June afternoon on Interstate 75, heading south in Juan's compact Jeep. They were glad that graduation had been scheduled for the morning so that they would have all afternoon to drive. Juan set the cruise control on 70 m.p.h., while Jose and Zac listened to their favorite CD's and drank their sodas.

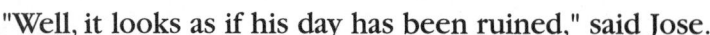

The six-hour drive went by quickly. Just before they reached Panama City, they saw a car wrapped around a telephone pole. State troopers, paramedics and a fire truck were close by. They slowed down as they passed, and the light bouncing off the vehicles caused the boys to squint.

"Well, it looks as if his day has been ruined," said Jose.

"Yeah! I feel sorry for him. He's not having any fun," added Zac. "I hope everybody is alright."

"Accidents like that always make me **skittish**," sighed Juan.

"Relax!" Zac said, with confidence.

"Yeah! You're right. Let's have fun!" agreed Juan.

22

All week, the boys attended one party after another, meeting a lot of fun and interesting people, while Jose played volleyball on the beach, and Zac hung out with a foreign exchange student named Sarieke. Juan was just content to soak up the rays and read.

On the night before their departure, they decided to take a cruise aboard a luxury cruise ship. Right before sunset, as a gorgeous array of colors bounced off the horizon, they set sail. As the night fell and the ship made its way up the coastline, the waves became unusually choppy.

Jose could not tolerate the **chaotic** rocking of the ship and he quickly became seasick. He went outside on the deck, instead of going to the dance. After a while, Jose was feeling better and decided he would rejoin the party. He stood up and tried to make his way back inside. However, as he was walking along the deck, a huge wave shifted the ship and sent Jose overboard. His loud screams and yells attracted only a few people's attention before he was sucked under the **turbulent** water.

As soon as Zac and Juan heard what happened, they rushed to the side of the ship and tried desperately to spot Jose in the dark water. Instead, they saw only the choppy water and white-capped waves. By then everyone was on the deck, watching and waiting. Suddenly, someone heard Jose screaming for help. At that moment, Zac caught a glimpse of him and jumped into the dangerous water. Zac was confident and had always been an **extraordinary** swimmer. He wasn't about to let his friend drown.

After about fifteen minutes, Zac managed to pull Jose to the ship's side and both were **hoisted** aboard safely. Zac was **fatigued** and out of breath, while Jose was shivering from cold, fear and shock. Eventually, everyone returned to the party except for Zac, Juan, and Jose, who wanted to stay together.

The next morning leaving Panama City, Juan was once again driving while Zac and Jose were listening to their CD's. As they passed the last part of the beach, they reflected on their graduation trip and the strengthened bond of friendship the three now shared. They looked at each other and could only smile.

READING CHALLENGE

After reading "Graduation!," answer the following questions.

Working with Vocabulary

Write the meaning for each word below.

1. skittish _____

2. chaotic _____

3. turbulent _____

4. extraordinary _____

5. hoisted _____

6. fatigued _____

Finding Details

7. From what city do the boys leave to travel to Panama City?

8. What was the name of the exchange student that Zac met on the beach?

9. Who drove the Jeep to Florida?

10. Describe the accident the boys saw on their vacation.

11. Who fell overboard the luxury cruise ship?

12. Which one of the boys is the extraordinary swimmer?

Sequencing the Events

13. Number the sentences in the order in which they occurred in the story.

_____ However, as he was walking along the deck a huge wave shifted the ship and sent Jose overboard.

_____ They left Atlanta on Interstate 75, heading south.

_____ Suddenly, someone heard Jose screaming for help.

_____ Right before sunset, as a gorgeous array of colors bounced off the horizon, they set sail.

_____ They slowed down as they passed, and the light bouncing off the vehicles caused all three boys to squint.

_____ Juan set the cruise control on 70 mph.

Checking Grammar

Right before sunset, as a gorgeous array of colors bounced off the horizon, they set sail.

14. What is the subject? _____

15. What type of phrase is <u>watching a gorgeous array of colors bouncing off the horizon</u>?

16. What part of speech is <u>before</u>?

24   Total Correct _____

CHAPTERS

Lola Mildred McPherson slowly awoke and was greeted by the bright sun rays of a new day. Sue, her roommate at Sunny Valley Nursing Home, was still snoring softly. Today was going to be a special day. Lola's granddaughter, Emily, would be making her weekly visit. Lola quickly made it through her breakfast and waited patiently until it was finally 10:00 a.m. Nothing could dampen her excitement, not even the loud, **indistinguishable** noises from the kitchen down the hallway.

She had thirty minutes to prepare for her visitor. Lola walked over to the mirror and peered in. Once a smooth face, sparkling eyes and long, dark hair would have stared back at her. However, now all she could see was the gray hair and wrinkles she had collected over her lifetime. Slowly, she powdered her face and brushed her hair. Suddenly, she was startled by a loud knock on the door.

Lola slowly walked over to the door and opened it to find Emily standing there smiling. She truly regretted not having her own home at times like these, because at home she could cook Emily a nice lunch, or invite her to stay the night. Emily, who had just turned thirteen, took a seat on the end of Lola's bed. They exchanged talk about Emily's family and then began doing what they had frequently done since Emily was ten years old. Emily listened as Lola continued to reveal the chapters of her life. Today she began with her marriage.

Lola closed her eyes and smiled as though her memories were an old friend. "Your grandpa, Emily, was a handsome man. We had been courting for about a year when he asked me to marry him. I remember it so vividly. I was a pretty young thing, about eighteen years old, when I met John Patrick at school. Let's see, this is 1999, so that would have been about 65 years ago.

CHAPTERS, *continued*

Anyway, John and I hit it off right away. We would go to socials and picnics together—that's where everyone went on dates back then. We were at one of those picnics when John dropped down on one knee, asked for my hand in marriage, and gave me a ring. It was a small opal. He didn't have much money, but then no one did. I was as happy as a lark. We asked my parents and they were agreeable, so we married on April 15, 1934, the day after my eighteenth birthday and six weeks after the proposal."

"We had a very small wedding. My family and I rode up to the church together; some relatives and a few friends were already there. Everyone had on their Sunday best. My dress was a soft white satin with a short train and a lace collar."

"After the ceremony, we went to our new home in John's finest buggy. The house was warm and simple—two things we both appreciated. John had built the house with his own two hands. I just loved it! My dad helped us begin our little farm by giving us some chickens, a cow, and a few other supplies as wedding presents."

"That summer and fall we worked **industriously** so that after about a year, we were able to begin saving some money. In July, I discovered that I was expecting our first child, and John wanted our children to have all the best we could give them. I went into labor on March 19th. All I remember is looking up and seeing my mother with a smile on her face and a tear on her cheek. She placed a warm, tiny bundle on my chest, and I saw my little boy. He was your father, and I named him Andrew Johnathan Davis. Your grandfather was so proud he almost busted his buttons!"

"All of our friends and relatives raved about what a pretty baby your father was. His **escapades** naturally got him into the worst trouble, but I reckoned that boys will be boys!"

After kissing Lola's wrinkled forehead and promising to return the next week, Emily reluctantly left. That night, Lola drifted off to sleep already dreaming of the next chapter of her life that she would tell Emily when she came to visit again.

26

Name ....

READING CHALLENGE

After reading "Chapters," circle the best answer in each question.

1. **The story is mainly about**
   A. a nursing home.
   B. the marriage of two people.
   C. building a home.
   D. memories.

2. **Where is the setting of the story?**
   A. nursing home in 1999
   B. school in 1934
   C. farm in 1998
   D. wedding in 1934

3. **Who was Andrew Johnathan Davis?**
   A. Emily's great uncle
   B. Emily's grandmother's son
   C. Emily's grandfather
   D. Emily's dad

4. **What is another word for <u>industriously</u>?**
   A. insignificantly
   B. diligently
   C. slightly
   D. sadly

5. **Which happened last?**
   A. Emily listened as Lola revealed chapter after chapter of her life.
   B. After the brief ceremony, we went to our new home in John's finest buggy.
   C. Lola drifted off to sleep dreaming of the next chapter of her life that she would tell Emily.
   D. We asked our parents and they were agreeable, so we married.

6. **His <u>escapades</u> would naturally get him into the worst trouble! <u>Escapades</u> means**
   A. pranks.
   B. solutions.
   C. friends.
   D. charms.

7. **How old was Lola when she married John Patrick?**
   A. sixty-four
   B. thirteen
   C. twenty-one
   D. eighteen

8. **John and Lola loved their first new home because it was**
   A. cool and simple.
   B. small and simple.
   C. warm and simple.
   D. warm and big.

9. **<u>Indistinguishable</u> means**
   A. alike.
   B. unclear.
   C. unmistakable.
   D. distinct.

Total Correct _____

27

The Bald Eagle

The bald eagle is the national symbol for the United States of America. However, most Americans do not know much about this **majestic** bird. For instance, the eagle's diet is quite varied.

It exists on different sources of food, including animals like fish, rodents, birds, snakes, monkeys, and rabbits. The eagle may eat **carrion**, but more often, it catches and eats fresh fish. To catch fish, the eagle may use one of several techniques. For example, it may circle in the air until it sees a fish and then dive into the water. However, it also may wade into shallow water and spear a fish with its beak, or may even steal a freshly caught fish from another bird.

If there are no fish available, the bald eagle may turn to waterfowl, such as ducks and geese, for its meal. Again, the **technique** the bald eagle uses in catching its prey is one of several. It may simply fly down, pounce on its prey, and fly away. It may force a duck or other diving bird to keep diving until it becomes exhausted and is easily caught, or the eagle may use the amazing technique of "catching a goose on the wing," which means catching the goose in full flight. To do this, the eagle dives under the goose and attacks from underneath, sinking its sharp **talons** into the breast of the goose.

Another interesting thing about the bald eagle is that it mates for life. The pair will often use the same nest year after year, adding new material to the nest each year. The largest nest on record is twenty feet deep and almost ten feet across. The eagle's nest, or aerie, is high in a tree or on a rocky ledge where it cannot be reached by other animals, a **precaution** that is necessary because young eagles remain helpless for long periods of time.

The female eagle generally lays one to three brownish, speckled eggs a year with either both parents or just the female incubating the eggs. The female usually feeds the young. The babies, covered with down, remain in the nest from 50 to 100 days. The young do not develop adult coloration until they are more than two years old.

Eagles are noted for their strength and keen vision. Most eagles range from two to three feet long and have wingspans of about six feet. One of the smallest, however, is only about sixteen inches long. The largest eagle reaches 39 inches in length with wingspans of up to eight feet.

Eagles have different distinguishing feather patterns. The bald eagle is really not bald. It was really named for its white head, while the rest of its **plumage** is brown. Although some eagles have a ring of pointed feathers around the head, others, called booted eagles, have feathers on their legs that go all the way to their talons.

Name ....

READING CHALLENGE

After reading "The Bald Eagle," answer the following questions.

Working with Vocabulary

The answers to the vocabulary words are found in a dictionary or in the story.

1. A word that means "the claws of a bird," is _____.

2. The "decaying flesh of animals," is the definition of _____.

3. A synonym for a word that means "foresight," is _____.

4. A word that means "having or showing stateliness or great dignity," is _____.

5. "A procedure or method for accomplishing a task," is the definition for _____.

6. A word meaning "the covering of feathers on a bird," is _____.

Finding Details

7. The longest known nest ever measured was ___ feet deep and ___ feet across.

8. What is the irony in the name of the bald eagle?

9. Where is the eagle's nest or aerie normally built?

10. What is the largest wingspan for the bald eagle?

11. Normally how long do young eagles remain in the nest?

12. The bald eagle's prey includes _____.

13. The bald eagle is the _____ _____ for the United States of America.

14. The female eagle generally lays how many eggs and what color are the eggs?

15. List one way that an eagle can catch a fish.

Total Correct _____ 29

THE ACCIDENT

As I drive home from work late on a Saturday night, the rain is cascading down in sheets. Cars speed past me as the glare of their headlights make it impossible for me to see. I'm driving around a sharp curve when I am blinded by an intensely bright light. My car skids out of control and is hurled off the road. I cannot regain control. Immediately, my world explodes into vivid colors and dissolves into blackness. The car is tumbling over and over. My head is spinning. My mind fills with visions from the past ...

Suddenly, I am a young girl sitting around the fire with my family, feeling **overwhelmed** by their love. Then, I am a teenager and it is summer, my favorite time of the year. The days are hot, but the nights are even hotter. At thirteen, my friends and I rule the town. I meet a guy who makes my heart skip a beat, but I cannot express my feelings. Too shy to tell him, I return to school wondering if I will ever see him again.

The car eventually stops rolling. My eyes are closed. My world remains a vortex. I can vaguely comprehend someone awkwardly pulling me from the car. Minutes seem to go by like seconds. I can hear the shrieking of sirens and people frantically shouting, but they seem distant and **incoherent**. I am being gently lifted onto a boat. All of my best friends are with me. The sun is glaring off the sparkling blue lake as we cruise across the water. The wind is gently blowing and the sun is scorching, but I am freezing as I ride along in what I assume is an emergency ambulance. I feel **lethargic.** My eyelids are too heavy to open. I'm trying to see, but blackness still envelopes me. Then, there is ...

... a guy. He seems extraordinarily familiar because he makes my heart race. I remember him. He is the guy I met when I was only thirteen. At sixteen, we date and he kisses me for the first time.

I hear a tender voice saying, "I love you. You're going to be okay." Making another determined attempt to open my eyes, I slowly focus on the world around me. I am staring into those same soft, beautiful brown eyes that I remember so well. They belong to the man who grew from the boy of my memories. The hospital room comes clearly into focus and becomes my reality as I look into the worried faces of my friends and family. Then, as I look into those big brown eyes of his, I realize how much I love him.

Fading before I have a chance to say anything, I drift off to sleep with him **caressing** my hand and standing very close to me.

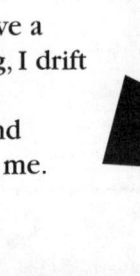

READING CHALLENGE

After reading "The Accident," answer the following questions.

1. What is the main idea of this story?

2. Place the sentences below in the sequence in which they occurred.
   _____ At thirteen, my friends and I rule the town.
   _____ My car skids out of control and is hurled off the road.
   _____ I'm trying to see, but blackness still envelopes me.
   _____ I can hear the shrieking of sirens and people frantically shouting. . . .
   _____ The hospital room comes clearly into focus and becomes my reality . . . .
   _____ Sitting around the fire with my family.

3. What is actually happening to the narrator of the story?
   A. She and her friends have been in a boating accident on the lake.
   B. She has been in a car accident and is fading in and out of consciousness.
   C. She has been in a car accident and her relatives are not with her.
   D. She and her friends have been in a car accident on a hot summer night.

4. The story suggests that the man who is caressing her hand in the hospital is
   A. her son.   B. her dad.   C. her husband.   D. her doctor.

Finding Details

5. At what age did she rule the town?

6. When did the extraordinary guy kiss her for the first time?

7. On which night of the week does the accident occur?

8. How does the reader know that the speaker in the story is a girl?

9. The reader is led to believe that the man in the hospital room is the same person she met when she was how old?

Working with Vocabulary

10. A word in the story that means <u>overcome</u> is _____.

11. A word that means <u>lacking logical connections</u> is _____.

12. A word that means <u>drowsy or sluggish indifference</u> is _____.

13. A word in the story that means <u>a gentle touch</u> is _____.

Total Correct _____   31

The Rose

I did not know how long I had been walking. After the disagreement with my mother, I just needed to get away and cool off. Suddenly, I awoke from my deep thoughts to find myself staring across the field at the old Johnson house.

I had never strayed this far away from home before and decided that I'd better head back, but my feet seemed glued to the ground and my eyes to the house. The Johnson house was a mystery to everyone although the mystery was not actually in the house, but the field beside the house. Every spring the most beautiful flowers would grow there. They were not wildflowers, but flowers that have to be planted and cared for every year. Nobody knew why, and none of my friends were brave enough to go near the old, **dilapidated** house to investigate for themselves.

Rumor had it that many years ago a mother and her baby fell down the stairs and were killed in a freak accident while her husband was working at the train yard. The husband discovered the bodies of his family when he returned that night, but soon died himself from the despair and loneliness of losing his family.

I suddenly felt an **uncontrollable** bout of curiosity when my foot stepped off the road and into the field of flowers. As I walked, my hands lightly touched the flowers and felt the beauty in their silky soft touch. As I neared the house, my heart began to pound as if I expected someone to jump out. Finally, I reached the house and stood before its rickety front porch. My foot trembled as I placed it on the first step. I lifted the other one and the step creaked, scaring me half to death! With great care, I made it up the steps one by one, and to the door, opening it slowly and stepping inside. It slammed behind me and I nearly jumped out of my skin. Recovering and beginning to scan the room, I seemed to be in what once was a living room. I walked around and looked, but for some reason I felt that to touch anything would be an **intrusion**. "What really happened here so many years ago?" was the question that went through my mind.

I spotted the infamous staircase and **ascended** it slowly. I walked down the hall and peered into a room. I could have fainted! There in front of the window was a woman. Ghost or human, I don't know, but I wasn't about to stay around and find out! I screamed and ran for the door! My leg hit the corner of the banister and I fell to the floor. My heart raced and my knees shook with adrenaline. I covered my face to hide from whatever was making its way toward me. With great fear, I reached out to see if she was real, but all I felt was cold air brushing against my face and then she was gone.

I jumped to my feet and ran down the stairs and out the door. I did not stop until I was well out of the house. When I got into the field of flowers, I looked back. Had I imagined it all? I looked at the house and there she was. "I have one thing to say to you," she said. "Always be kind to your mother, for she will always love you." She handed me a rose and disappeared. All the way home I just stared at the most beautiful rose I had ever seen. It would be perfect to give to my mother.

READING CHALLENGE

After reading "The Rose," fill in the correct answer bubble.

1. The story is mainly about
   - A. a freak accident.
   - B. picking flowers.
   - C. suspicion and kindness.
   - D. disagreements with sister.

2. <u>Dilapidated</u> means
   - A. run down.
   - B. perfect.
   - C. antique.
   - D. renovated.

3. What had happened in the house?
   - A. a woman fell down the stairs
   - B. a man had fallen down the stairs
   - C. a woman grew old
   - D. a woman & baby fell down the stairs

4. Why is the narrator walking in the fields?
   - A. because of a disagreement with mother
   - B. wanted to pick flowers
   - C. to get away and think
   - D. an uncontrollable bout of curiosity

5. An <u>intrusion</u> means
   - A. inspection
   - B. investigation
   - C. safeguard
   - D. invasion

6. How did the narrator obtain the rose?
   - A. a male "ghost"
   - B. a female "ghost"
   - C. the narrator picked it
   - D. the narrator found it

7. Which happened first?
   - A. I walked down the hall and peered into a room.
   - B. but soon died himself from the despair and loneliness....
   - C. the mystery was not actually in the house....
   - D. When I got into the fields of flowers, I looked back.

8. I spotted a staircase and <u>ascended</u> it slowly. <u>Ascended</u> means
   - A. climbed.
   - B. descended.
   - C. sank.
   - D. tripped.

9. The flowers suggest that
   - A. someone has a green thumb.
   - B. someone likes wildflowers.
   - C. someone likes gardening.
   - D. someone lives in the house.

Remember, if you don't know what a word means, look it up in a dictionary! You'll do better in the exercises!

Total Correct _____   33

Coming Home

As Daniel looked out of the airplane window, he began to think of the last time that he had seen his son, Randy. It had been four long years since Daniel had been home to Washington, D.C. Daniel had attended the Naval Academy and was then required to spend four years on an overseas assignment. He had spent most of those four years in the Middle East.

Daniel's mind was **preoccupied** with thoughts of his son and his wife, Monica. During his time in the Middle East, he had the opportunity to see his family in the family video they sent him once a month. As Daniel thought about his little boy, he found it inconceivable to think about how much he had grown. Randy would be five in a month and Daniel was going to be there to help him celebrate. The joy he felt at that moment was both **indescribable** and **unimaginable**.

Presently, the pilot announced over the intercom, "This is your captain speaking. Please fasten your seat belts. We will be arriving in Miami shortly. This will be our last stop before flying on to Washington, D.C."

Daniel's thoughts turned to Friday, when he and his family would meet the President. Daniel was being awarded a medal of honor for his bravery in an encounter with an enemy vessel. He had also been asked to be the Grand Marshall of a parade planned to march from the White House to the Lincoln Memorial.

Daniel **retrieved** a book from his carry-on bag just as his plane touched down on the runway. He waited patiently as the passengers staying in Miami exited the plane. After about thirty minutes, the plane began to move again. Exhausted from the already lengthy trip, he decided to rest, closing his eyes. He drifted off to sleep thinking, "Two more hours. I can hardly wait."

Suddenly, the tense voice of the captain over the intercom awoke Daniel. "This is your captain speaking. We have terrorists aboard the plane. They are armed, so please remain seated and do exactly as they say."

Suddenly, the door from the cockpit flew open and three men in ski masks emerged. One remained in the cockpit, another stayed in the front of the plane, while the third man with a briefcase went to the back of the plane. Daniel suspected that the briefcase contained some type of explosive. Daniel was trained to deal with situations like this and knew he must wait.

After what seemed to be an eternity, Daniel saw the man at the front of the plane turn away slightly. He knew this might be his only chance, so he leapt from his seat and quickly tackled the masked man from behind, wrestling him to the floor. A nearby flight attendant **retrieved** the terrorist's weapon which had fallen from his hand during the brawl.

Daniel knew he had to move quickly. Stepping into the aisle, he saw the terrorist from the cockpit rush through the door. After a quick skirmish, Daniel rendered the man unconscious with a blow to the head. This time a nearby passenger grabbed the terrorist's weapon and waved to Daniel to let him know he had it under control.

Daniel now made his way to the back of the plane where he saw the third terrorist's legs sticking out into the aisle. Above him stood a huge professional wrestler who apparently did not like being threatened! With cat-like quickness, the wrestler had grabbed the terrorist, spun him above his head and had taken him down into a full nelson! Daniel smiled at the wrestler who gave him a "thumbs up," sign. Now it was up to Daniel to find the bomb.

Using lessons he had learned through military training, Daniel guessed that the terrorist had planted the bomb in the bathroom. Rushing to the bathroom, he found the briefcase, but no bomb! Daniel began to disassemble the bathroom at a frantic pace. He found what he was looking for! The explosives were stuffed inside the paper towel dispenser!

Daniel looked at the timer and realized that they had five minutes before the bomb would explode. What was going to happen? What must he do?

35

READING CHALLENGE

After reading "Coming Home," answer the following questions.

1. The story is mainly about

2. After reading the story, write an appropriate ending.

3. Describe an unpredictable or unsafe situation that you have been in.

Working with Vocabulary

4. A word in the story that means <u>distracted</u> is _____.

5. A word that means <u>regained</u> or <u>recovered</u> is _____.

6. <u>Impossible to describe</u> is the meaning for _____.

7. A word in the story that means <u>unbelievable</u> is _____.

Finding Details

8. Where was the bomb found? _____

9. Where is Daniel's home located? _____

10. For the past four years, Daniel has been stationed in what area? _____

11. How long has it been since Daniel has seen his son, Randy? _____

12. How many terrorists were aboard the plane? _____

13. When Daniel finds the bomb, how many minutes are left before it explodes? _____

Total Correct _____

36

End of the Night

Under the thick blanket of midnight
the wind is cool on my face.
With one of my senses gone
things become a little clearer.
For some reason the trees act angry,
and they seem to be awake.
They whisper nature's secret amongst themselves
and I just walk on in ignorance.

Night skies become clear
and the moon has arrived with light.
I can see, now, how the frightened grass
is being **intimidated** by the wind,
which moves hurriedly on its way.
The stars seem to be speaking
words my ears cannot hear.
At least, that is what I feel inside.

Suddenly, the East has exploded,
bringing forth a blossom of red-orange and pink.
The moon has departed and taken the darkness with it,
for the sun is now caressing the countryside.
The dew, which the grass must endure,
slowly takes flight, to kiss some foreign acre.
And skies, turned blue with content,
carry the ghosts which take the wind for granted.

READING CHALLENGE

After reading "End of the Night," fill in the correct answer bubble.

1. The poem is mainly about
   - A. nature's secrets.
   - B. night skies.
   - C. the beginning of summer.
   - D. the ending of a night.

2. . . . **intimidated** by the wind means
   - A. fear.
   - B. encouraged.
   - C. helped.
   - D. damaged.

3. "They whisper nature's secret . . ." is an example of a
   - A. pun.
   - B. personification.
   - C. simile.
   - D. metaphor.

Total Correct _____

Is There Really An Atlantis?

Juan had just graduated from college with a degree in **oceanography**. The sea fascinated him. One clear, hot summer day, Juan and his team were mapping the Pacific Ocean floor off the coast of Chile in South America. Juan decide to go down in his one-man submarine to examine the ocean floor. As he was lowered into the sea, Juan was awe-struck by the beauty and mystery of the oceanic world around him.

After reaching a depth of 2,000 feet, he unhooked his sub from the safety cable and decided to explore on his own. To the right, he noticed a **grotto** that was partially hiding a sunken submarine. Curious about this unexpected find, Juan decided to explore the old wreckage. He quickly put on his wet suit and exited the sub. He reached the submarine and found the hatch covered with a slimy moss. After scraping the moss away, he pried the hatch open and lowered himself into the mysterious vessel.

To his surprise, the inside was perfectly clean. It almost appeared to be inhabited by living humans—but this was impossible! He searched around but found no clues, so he went back to the one-man sub. Back inside his sub, Juan turned on the big spotlight for a more intense **exploration** of the sunken submarine's exterior. Suddenly, the light fell upon a big, metal door in the rear. He was suspicious as he examined the door in the spotlight. Juan hurriedly left his tiny ship to get a closer look. As he felt his way around the door, he tried numerous times to open it, but failed every time. As he was leaving, Juan jokingly knocked on the door. As if by magic, the door slowly, almost painfully, creaked open. He was **astounded**!

Slowly, he made his way inside. As his eyes focused, he saw three people walking toward him from the depths of the ship. As they approached, Juan and this group exchanged **inquiring** glances. They invited Juan to stay a while in the entrance chamber and listen to their story. They told him that he had discovered the lost city of Atlantis, which had been swallowed by the sea many centuries ago. The wrecked sub had been found by a group of Atlanteans who were on a fishing expedition in the deep waters of the ocean. The Atlantean people had voted to preserve the sub as a souvenir of the upper world.

Juan was invited to come with them to their underwater city but, if he did, he could never return to his own world. Juan was tempted by this offer, but decided that he could not leave his home above the sea.

Reading Challenge

After reading "Is There Really An Atlantis?," circle the best answer for each question.

1. The story is mainly about
   A. fishing off the coast of Chile.
   B. exploring the coral reefs.
   C. discovering the lost city, Atlantis.
   D. the study of oceanography.

2. The location of the story is in
   A. North America.
   B. South America.
   C. South Africa.
   D. South Asia.

3. Exploration means
   A. an investigation.
   B. an explanation.
   C. an opening.
   D. a renovation.

4. In which body of water does this expedition take place?
   A. Atlantic Ocean
   B. Black Sea
   C. Indian Ocean
   D. Pacific Ocean

5. What was surprising about the inside of the mysterious vessel?
   A. it was dark and dirty
   B. it was perfectly clean
   C. it was uninhabited
   D. it was well-lit and decorated

6. Astounded means
   A. shocked.
   B. unamazed.
   C. unconcerned.
   D. agitated.

7. What purpose does the sunken sub serve?
   A. underwater study facility
   B. floating restaurant
   C. souvenir of the upper world
   D. base for lost divers

8. He noticed a grotto partially hiding a sunken submarine. Grotto means
   A. building.
   B. statue.
   C. aircraft carrier.
   D. cave.

9. How many Atlanteans did Juan see on the mysterious submarine?
   A. 2000
   B. 3
   C. 20
   D. 200

10. Actually, what is Atlantis?
    A. lost submarine
    B. lost oceanography lab
    C. lost city
    D. lost ship

11. The meaning of oceanography is
    A. the study of the ocean.
    B. the study of the sea creatures.
    C. the study of plants.
    D. the study of submarines.

Total Correct _____

The Key

Hannah walked down the crowded street on the way to meet her husband. It was an especially cold winter, and everyone was bundled up in warm coats. Children, running in circles, were trying to catch snowflakes on their tongues. In the distance, Hannah could hear the **harmonious** voices of Christmas carolers. As the sweet songs filled the air, she drifted back to the memories of a Christmas long ago.

It was the year she was sixteen, the oldest of three children. Their father had always worked hard to make Christmas a special time for his children. Their mother had died in a car accident when Hannah was very young, and she could hardly remember her. This year, however, was going to be even more special. This was the year Hannah would receive the key to a box that had belonged to her mother.

Even as a little girl, Hannah had spent hours gazing at it, **fantasizing** about its contents. The **mystique** and allure of the box had not **diminished** with time. Sometimes she imagined that it housed a beautiful ring with sparkling emeralds and diamonds. At other times, she imagined a majestic necklace of dazzling gems–rubies, sapphires, and amethysts–all nestled in its embrace. Once she even **envisioned** a glamorous pendant of pure gold.

When the day finally arrived, Hannah was dizzy with excitement. She sat impatiently on the sofa as her father handed her the miniature key. She eagerly placed the key in the lock. As the key slowly turned the lock, she realized just how beautiful the box really was. Her mind was flooded with faint memories of her mother and her wild imagination. She had been waiting for this moment a long time.

Gently, she lifted the lid off the box and instantly focused on what lay inside. It finally belonged to her! Before her mother died, she had requested that Hannah receive this gift when she was old enough. Hannah's heart was filled with joy and love as she gazed at this wondrous gift. Beautiful and pure, it was a picture of her mother sealed in a golden locket on a chain.

READING CHALLENGE

After reading "The Key," circle the best answer for each question.

Working with Vocabulary

Write the meaning for each word.

1. harmonious _____

2. envisioned _____

3. mystique _____

4. diminished _____

5. fantasizing _____

Finding Details

6. What had happened to Hannah's mother?

7. What was the mother's request?

8. How old was Hannah when her mother died?

9. What did Hannah find in the box?

10. Who is the speaker or narrator in the story, a woman or a sixteen-year old girl?

11. The story takes place at what time of the year?

Sequencing the Story

12. Number the sentences in the order in which they occurred in the story.

___ Their mother had died in a car accident when Hannah was very young. . . .

___ Children, running in circles, were trying to catch snowflakes on their tongues.

___ Once she even envisioned a glamorous pendant of pure gold.

___ As the sweet songs filled the air, she drifted back to the memories of a Christmas. . . .

___ Gently, she lifted the lid off the box and instantly focused on what lay inside.

___ As the key slowly turned the lock, she realized just how beautiful the box really was.

Reading to Write

13. Discuss or describe something of special value that has been given to you from a loved one.

Total Correct _____

The Race of a Lifetime

Andy was preparing for the 500-mile dog sled race to Nome. He had traveled from Salem, Washington to Anchorage, Alaska earlier that day. Even though it was his first time at the race, he felt ready. Andy had wanted to participate in this race for as long as he could remember and had saved enough money to buy a decent sled and twenty good dogs. The race would begin in forty-eight hours. Andy did not have much time to adjust to the cold, harsh climate or to get his supplies packed onto his sled. However, that did not matter to Andy. He knew this would be the ultimate thrill of his life.

Later, he checked into a local hotel that maintained a kennel for the dog sled teams in the race. After he took care of his dogs for the night, Andy retired to his room. As soon as his head hit the soft pillow he fell into a deep, dreamless sleep.

The next morning, the loud clamor of the street below awoke young Andy from his sleep. Within five minutes, he was dressed and out the door for his first day in the snowy city of Anchorage. Before he went walking, he checked and fed his dogs. He paid careful attention to all of his dogs, especially his lead dog. His lead dog, Ace, had become Andy's faithful and loving companion during the five years they had been together. After visiting the dogs, he went to the store and bought the food that he would need for the next two weeks out in the wilderness.

Later in the evening when Andy returned to the hotel, he packed the remainder of his equipment and tightly fastened the latches on the long sled. He checked on his dogs one last time before retiring.

The next morning, Andy was up early and had assembled his sled before most of the racers had even gotten out of bed. Within an hour, however, the street was filled with sleds, loud men, and shaggy dogs. As the announcer gave the signal for the 30 participants to line up along the starting line, Andy's heart began to race. He realized he was about to embark on the greatest challenge of his life. He was eighteen and ready to become a man. All of Andy's anxieties **dissipated** when the announcer pulled the trigger and the loud crack of the starter pistol echoed over the mountain ridges.

The thirty sleds roared as their skis were pulled across the hard snow by the dog teams. The shouts of men and the barking dogs only added to the mass confusion, with everyone trying to get out of town and into the open. Once the sleds reached the open field of snow, the crowd of racers scattered and Andy was able to make his own trail. Ace had made this trip a few times before and he pressed forward with confidence. They traveled directly north all day, using the sun to guide them. According to Andy's calculations, he estimated they had traveled more than thirty miles. He built his first night's camp in a patch of shrubs. Retiring early, he knew he must get some sleep, for he would need his strength the next day.

The next morning, Andy woke to the sunrise peeking out over the horizon. After preparing for the day ahead, he continued on his long journey through the winter landscape. Toward the late afternoon, Andy could tell a storm was forming in the clouds overhead. Within an hour, a fierce blizzard was upon them. He did the best he could to lead his pack to safety, finding a patch of trees to provide cover until the storm was over. Afterwards, he found a place to make camp for the night. He slept beside Ace, who kept him warm and comfortable throughout the night.

The next morning, Andy could tell they were off course and terribly lost. He kept his composure, trying not to upset the dogs. They continued moving north in hopes of finding other sled tracks. They were not successful. By nightfall, he calculated that they had traveled about forty-five miles. Before drifting off to sleep, he wrote an entry in the journal he had been keeping since his **journey** began.

Many days passed without signs of other travelers on the cold, barren plains of snow. By the end of the first week, Andy realized his food supplies were rapidly disappearing. Nevertheless, he found comfort in Ace's companionship.

During the second week, Andy's food ran out, forcing him to **forage** for food. To make matters worse, three of his dogs ran off looking for food one night. He assumed he was close enough to Nome, so the loss of the dogs would not matter that much. The sled traveled at a slightly slower speed now and with less power. Andy still hoped to win the race, but he knew that his chances were slim.

The Race of a Lifetime
continued

Andy arrived at a nearby pond and was astonished when he found an old fishing hook. He laced the hook with some string from his sleigh, broke through the ice, and set his line down in the icy waters. Within a few hours, he had caught several fish, enough to feed his team and himself for a few days.

In the next four days, Andy and his team walked close to a hundred miles, surviving on the fish he had caught. They had been walking in the same direction for days and still had not reached their destination in Nome.

Still several miles from his destination, another snowstorm forced Andy and the team to make camp for the evening. Andy collapsed in the snow, weak from hunger and despair. His **emaciated** frame shook with tears. His loyal dog, Ace, drew close in an attempt to console his master, but could only lay nearby as Andy drifted off into a fitful sleep. He had given up hope of ever winning the race.

When Andy awoke in the morning, Ace was barking excitedly. The falling snow that had obscured Andy's view the night before had cleared and Andy was able make out the outline of a little town on the horizon. A wave of relief washed over Andy's entire body. He knew that little town was Nome.

He crossed the finish line with the applause of the other sled drivers to cheer him on. Although Andy and his team were not the first to cross the finish line, Andy knew that what they had accomplished was worth more than a trophy or prize money. The fact that they had finished the race was a victory that Andy would carry in his heart for the rest of his life, and so would the people of Nome.

READING CHALLENGE

After reading "The Race of a Lifetime," circle the best answer for each question.

1. The story is mainly about
    A. dog sled racing.
    B. cold weather of the Arctic.
    C. accepting challenges.
    D. taking care of dogs.

2. <u>Odyssey</u> means
    A. journey.
    B. nightmare.
    C. dream.
    D. sickness.

3. The dog sled race began in
    A. Salem.
    B. Anchorage.
    C. Nome.
    D. Fairbanks.

4. Andy's faithful companion and lead dog was
    A. Nome.
    B. Hook.
    C. Arctic.
    D. Ace.

5. Andy's anxieties <u>dissipated</u> means
    A. his anxieties heightened.
    B. his anxieties disappeared.
    C. his anxieties increased.
    D. his anxieties grew.

6. What did Andy and his team eat when their food supply ran out?
    A. snow
    B. fish
    C. rabbit
    D. squirrel

7. Andy came from
    A. Salem, Washington.
    B. Chicago, Illinois.
    C. Washington, D.C..
    D. Fairbanks, Alaska.

8. <u>Emaciated</u> means
    A. well-nourished.
    B. gaunt.
    C. obese.
    D. healthy.

9. How many sleds were in the race?
    A. two
    B. sixty
    C. eighteen
    D. thirty

10. In the story, how old is Andy?
    A. twenty
    B. thirty
    C. eighteen
    D. twenty-eight

11. . . . to <u>forage</u> for food means
    A. to search.
    B. to grow.
    C. to throw away.
    D. to buy.

12. The story suggests that when Andy crossed the finish line, he felt
    A. proud that he made it.
    B. mad because he didn't win.
    C. confused about where he was .
    D. sad that his dogs had run off.

Remember, if you don't know what a word means, look it up in a dictionary! You'll do better in the exercises!

Total Correct _____

A Southern Christmas: An Essay

As Amy stood and watched her mother carefully place the last ornament on the tree, she thought about how wonderful this Christmas would be. Even though she was in the eighth grade, Amy still loved Christmas. Her sister would be coming home from college and all of her relatives would be coming to visit as well.

Amy could smell the **aroma** of the food her mother was preparing. Her mother always cooked enormous amounts of food for the holidays because there was such a large family to feed. She had seven cousins, three aunts, three uncles, two grandmothers, two grandfathers, and a great-grandmother. Occasionally, a few neighbors would also stop by.

The customary Christmas dinner was ham, sweet potato casserole, green beans, corn, and freshly baked bread. The smallest children ate hamburgers and french fries. Desserts were Amy's favorites: chocolate cake, peanut butter cookies, and caramel candy.

After dinner, the older members of the family would sit by the fireplace to drink eggnog and talk, while the very young went out to play. The adults would talk about the old days and Christmases past. Just before midnight, everyone would go to sleep. The children, who had been playing and enjoying themselves, were forced to go to bed. The adults explained to them that if they did not go to sleep, Santa would not come.

It never failed that on Christmas morning one of the young ones would wake at dawn and run through the house screaming, "Santa has come!" It didn't take long for the **commotion** to wake the entire house. After opening the gifts, the children would play with their toys while mother and grandmother prepared breakfast.

After an enjoyable breakfast, relatives packed their bags and headed for home. It was always a fun time, with lots of good food, laughter, love, and wonderful southern memories.

READING CHALLENGE

After reading "A Southern Christmas: An Essay," answer the following questions.

1. The essay is mainly about

2. Discuss how your area of the country celebrates Christmas.

3. Place the sentences in sequence as they occur in the essay.
   _____ It never failed that on Christmas morning one of the young ones . . . .
   _____ The smallest children ate hamburgers and french fries.
   _____ The children, who had been playing and enjoying themselves, were . . . .
   _____ Her mother always cooked enormous amounts of food for the holidays . . . .
   _____ After opening the gifts, the children would play with their toys . . . .
   _____ Even though she was in eighth grade, Amy still loved Christmas.

4. The customary Christmas dinner consisted of
   A. sweet potato casserole, green beans, corn, bread, and chicken.
   B. sweet potato casserole, green beans, corn, bread and ham.
   C. green beans, ham, sweet potato casserole, peas, and bread.
   D. corn, bread, ham, sweet potato casserole, and baked beans.

5. Amy had which of the following relatives?
   A. two aunts, seven cousins, three uncles, two grandmothers, two grandfathers
   B. six cousins, three uncles, three aunts, two grandmothers, two grandfathers
   C. one grandmother, two grandfathers, three aunts, three uncles, seven cousins
   D. seven cousins, three aunts, three uncles, two grandmothers, two grandfathers, and a great-grandmother

Finding Details

6. In the essay, about how old is Amy?

7. In what part of the country does the essay take place?

8. Why did the adults "force" the young children to go to bed on Christmas Eve?

Working with Vocabulary

9. Which word in the essay means "disturbance"?

10. Which word in the essay means "a pleasant, characteristic smell"?

Total Correct _____

Mad King Prey

My breathing is loud, yes, much too loud, for it will betray me. I must slow down and control it. The leaves also are no friend of mine; their crackling is worse than that of fire. The fire of many burning huts; and so many villages were brought to the ground like black faces on the forest floor. The smoke, which would befriend me this day, would be as a blanket to cover me, hiding me from those hunters. They chase me tirelessly, but I know I shall prove to be stronger.

The bird's song is as peaceful as a harp in the royal courts. I fancy myself among the elite rulers, an **oppressor** of the common people. All in my dungeon, I'd have 'em, a worthless lot. My subjects are the birds, and I, their king. How loyal they are to their kind master, singing the sweet music I hear, feel, even see on occasions, floating on the wind through the forest.

The forest is altogether its own wonder, like an emerald, as green as the ocean's water. Its trees stand as tall as stationary giants, their limbs keeping the sun from my face. The shadows conceal me, keeping the sun from my eyes. I am like a mother bear with her young. The birds tell their king of his **pursuers'** approach. Then I run on through this leafy emerald forest, a jewel worth much more than I have ever seen.

I find the forest to be like the wide ocean. Though I cannot swim, I have seen the ocean before with its great waves that are more powerful than any person. They are untamable and if they were not, I would make them my subjects, too. They would willingly wipe away my **adversaries**. Then the birds, my birds, would take flight and lift me to safety. This cannot be, I know, for the waves are under control of no one human being.

Perhaps though, these waves would aid me in my escape. They could bear me to a faraway place where I would be king of all. Birds would sing in my courts and all about my throne. The vines then would guard my gates and give no protection to the hunters who chase me so intently. Then, perhaps, I would become as they, and no longer play the role of **quarry**, while they would run with sweat steaming from their brow, and their breath would be loud, much too loud, betraying them.

Although I feel now that I must press on farther through the emerald forest, I know I can never defeat them until I have won my kingdom far across the green forest of water. The ground becomes rocky now, and the stones are allies to me, not as noisy as the evil leaves. My passing is not quite so evident and with care, they will lose me. My friends, the giant trees, are now fewer, but my birds have brought clouds to the sky to cover that flaming sphere.

I see now that the giants no longer travel with me. Could it be that they wait on my enemies to view their passing and tell me of their actions? Grass and rocks cover the land I cross now. The exposure doesn't frighten me terribly, though I feel a sense of uneasiness. I know my friends will protect me from their approach, for I smell the cool breezes of salt from my ocean. They can never be mine, I fear, but I know that to continue will lead me to the rocky cliffs, and below that, the waves will take me home.

Even now they are in sight, and a few more minutes will bring me to them. The sky is the gray color of wolves, much as I am, yet very different, as they run in packs. The gulls, my gulls, fly overhead to **divulge** my arrival to the ocean. I see the water's foam as it crashes to the rocks several feet below. A single leap will get me over into the sea's hands, safe from the enemies.

I know my gulls will catch their king so he will not hit the rocks. I pray thee, oh ocean, to take me home. What sweet sounds I hear as the air rushes upward, followed by the ocean, the waves and rocks, to receive me.

READING CHALLENGE

Name

After reading "Mad King Prey," answer the following questions.

Working with Vocabulary

The answer to the vocabulary words are found in the story or in a dictionary.

1. A word that means "prey," _____.

2. "To announce," is to _____.

3. A word that means "an unjust use of authority," _____.

4. "Enemies," are _____.

5. Another word for "ones who follow, hoping to overtake" is _____.

Finding Details

6. Why doesn't the Mad King consider the leaves to be his friend?

7. "The forest is altogether its own wonder like an emerald . . .." The expression "like an emerald," indicates what writing technique?

8. On what does the Mad King rely at the end to save him from enemies?

9. In the first paragraph, on what does the Mad King use as a cover for hiding and protection?

Sequencing the Story

10. Number the sentences in the order in which they occurred in the story.

_____ The exposure doesn't frighten me terribly, though I feel a sense . . . .

_____ The forest is altogether its own wonder, like an emerald . . . .

_____ They are untamable and if they were not, I would make them my subjects, too.

_____ I know my gulls will catch their king so he will not hit the rocks.

_____ My subjects are the birds, and I, their king.

_____ The ground becomes rocky now, and the stones are allies to me . . . .

Checking Grammar

The vines then would guard my gates and give no quarter to the hunters that chase me so intently.

11. What is the verb in the sentence?

12. What is the subject?

13. What part of speech is <u>then</u>?

14. Is the clause <u>that chase me so intently</u> independent or dependent?

Total Correct _____

My Eighth Grade English Journal

Tues., Oct. 20, 1998

Last Sunday, my grandpa died. He was the nicest man I have ever known. Of course, my dad is nice, but my grandpa was different and nice in another way. I already miss him terribly, and I don't know who I will be able to talk to the way I talked to him. He was my best friend, and always **heedful** of how I felt and of what I had to say. And best friends are difficult to find, especially this year. Eighth grade is fun, but I don't have a very best friend. Grandpa always said I had a great personality and that I would have lots of friends one day. However, I never cared because I had always had him. He was the only best friend I ever needed.

We never did anything special, just hung out together. When I went to his house, we would usually sit on the front porch, talking and listening to each other. If I had a problem, he would let me work it out, never telling me what I must do and how I must do it. He would just listen and eventually the answer would come. Grandpa should have been a teacher because he could have helped many students with their problems. A teacher should have an incredible amount of composure, like Grandpa did. I never heard him raise his voice, and he was very easy-going and patient.

Wed., Nov. 4, 1998

I am grounded and I am frustrated with my parents. Just because I didn't turn in a math assignment, they have grounded me for two days! I have never been able to do advanced math and algebra, especially now that Grandpa is gone, because he often helped me with my math. He made it so easy. My math teacher, Mrs. Finley, does not explain the reading problems to us. She just tells us to do them. All the students in our third period class think she needs to spend more time with us individually. Grandpa would ask me to read the problem, and then **summarize** the statement. Eventually, we would work out the problem together.

I hate being grounded because I can't talk on the telephone or watch television. I now have to spend more time doing math and algebra, and I have a tutor who comes over two nights a week. My tutor's name is Ted, a junior at Parkside High. He plays basketball. If I still had Grandpa though, I wouldn't need a tutor because he knew so much.

READING CHALLENGE

After reading "My Eighth Grade Journal," fill in the correct answer bubble.

1. In the sentence, "A teacher should have an incredible amount of composure," the word <u>incredible</u> means
   - A. amazing.
   - B. impossible.
   - C. unlikely.
   - D. unlawful.

2. Where did the student's tutor attend high school?
   - A. Sunday High School
   - B. Finley High School
   - C. Parkside High School
   - D. Park High School

3. Grandpa would ask me to read the problem, and then <u>summarize</u> the statement. In this sentence, summarize means
   - A. lengthen.
   - B. condense.
   - C. obscure.
   - D. unclear.

4. How does the speaker in the journal feel about the math teacher?
   - A. She and Grandpa are very much alike.
   - B. She is considered to be the best teacher in school.
   - C. She explains math problems carefully to all the students.
   - D. She needs to do better.

5. How old is the narrator in the journal?
   - A. does not say
   - B. eleven
   - C. fifteen
   - D. nine

6. In the sentence, "He was my best friend, always heedful," what does <u>heedful</u> mean?
   - A. helping occasionally
   - B. shirking responsibilities
   - C. paying close attention
   - D. not paying close attention

Total Correct _____

The Allure of South Dakota

Imagine sitting on Abraham Lincoln's nose or sunbathing on Thomas Jefferson's hairline! Well, you can at Mount Rushmore in South Dakota, where Abraham Lincoln, Thomas Jefferson, George Washington and Theodore Roosevelt are grandly presented as 465-foot tall stone carvings! These proud representations of America's great leaders were carved out of the granite face of the mountain by Gutzon Borglum. Today these majestic faces stand **resplendently** bathed in the South Dakota sun by day and radiantly illuminated by spotlight at night.

The carving began on August 10, 1927, and continued for fourteen years. However, the actual time spent working on the carvings was only about six and a half years because of weather delays and lack of money. This project took place during the Great Depression and cost a fortune by the standards of the time: $990,000. Borglum died in 1941, but his son, Lincoln, continued his life's work. However, this phenomenal stone memorial was never fully completed. Borglum had originally planned to show Washington to the waist with Lincoln gripping his collar in a stately pose. Additionally, he planned to hollow out a cavern in which he would display the history of American civilization.

Sculptor Korczak Ziokowski was so taken by the amazing stature of these carvings that he set out to create an even larger statue to honor Native Americans. This sculpture depicts the famous Sioux Indian, Crazy Horse, riding bareback on a magnificent horse. One can imagine the unbridled freedom of horse and rider, hear the pounding hoofs, and feel the rushing wind surge by while gazing up at this amazing statue. This giant stone **equestrian** will be the largest mountain carving in the world when it is completed. It is so large that all four presidential faces carved on Mount Rushmore could fit into Crazy Horse's head! This extraordinary effort is being funded solely by private donations and the money collected from admission fees paid by the thousands of tourists who flock to see it each year. The Native American organization sponsoring this incredible effort has declined U.S. government funding in tribute to the philosophy of Crazy Horse, the brave Native American leader it represents.

South Dakota's largest town, Sioux Falls, was once quarried for pink, red and lavender quartz. This quartz was used for constructing buildings and paving streets. At the turn of the century, skilled stonecutters were brought in from Scandinavia, Scotland and Wales to cut and polish quartz to be crafted into tabletops, jewelry, and picture frames. Early on, the most famous retail outlet for Sioux Falls quartz was Tiffany's in New York.

The Allure of South Dakota, *continued*

Legend has it that in 1879, Richard Pittigrew dammed the river upstream from Sioux Falls to fool a prospective investor, George Seney, from New Jersey. Just before Seney's arrival, Pettigrew had the dam removed so that the water would roar over the falls, convincing Mr. Seney there was enough water to power a flour mill. Pettigrew's deception worked. When completed, the Queen Bee Mill stood seven stories tall. The mill produced 1,200 barrels of flour daily until it closed two years later due to a drought. However, in the end, the joke was on Pettigrew. Without rain there was neither wheat crops to mill nor enough water flowing down the river to power the mill!

South Dakota is a state filled with natural and man-made places of interest for both natives and visitors alike. It is rich in the history of Native Americans, and filled with tales of precious gold and stories of the wild West.

South Dakota includes the incredible Badlands — miles of nearly barren land and the habitat of numerous desert animals and plants.

Each year the **allure** of South Dakota brings thousands of visitors from all over the world to explore the wonders of this beautiful state. Perhaps someday you will want to experience the fascination of South Dakota in person.

READING CHALLENGE

After reading "The Allure of South Dakota," fill in the correct answer bubble.

1. "Each year the allure of South Dakota brings thousands of visitors from . . . ." Allure means
    - A. dissatisfaction.
    - B. contempt.
    - C. attraction.
    - D. abhorrence.

2. Which American President is not represented in Mount Rushmore?
    - A. Abraham Lincoln
    - B. George Washington
    - C. Thomas Jefferson
    - D. Andrew Jackson

3. The famous Crazy Horse Memorial is a tribute to
    - A. a brave Native American.
    - B. Mount Rushmore.
    - C. George Seney.
    - D. Sioux Falls.

4. The word resplendent means
    - A. brilliant.
    - B. colored.
    - C. touring.
    - D. lonely.

5. Why does the Native American organization sponsoring the Crazy Horse Memorial decline government funding?
    - A. does not need the money
    - B. to remain free from government support
    - C. to remain free from political interest
    - D. as a tribute to the philosophy of Crazy Horse

6. "This realistic stone equestrian will be . . . ." Equestrian means
    - A. a person dressed as a horse.
    - B. a person who feeds a horse.
    - C. a person who rides a horse.
    - D. a person who herds horses.

7. ". . . . miles of barren land and habitat of numerous desert animals and plants," is a description of
    - A. Sioux Falls.
    - B. Black Hills.
    - C. Badlands.
    - D. Queen Bee Mill.

8. The actual time spent carving Mount Rushmore was approximately how many years?
    - A. six and a half
    - B. seven and a half
    - C. fourteen
    - D. seven

9. The largest mountain carving in the world when completed will be
    - A. Mount Rushmore.
    - B. Sioux Falls.
    - C. Queen Bee Mill.
    - D. Crazy Horse.

Total Correct _____

Marley the Magician

Once upon a time, there was a young man of thirteen years who loved to paint. He **perpetually** drew, painted, and daydreamed about becoming a famous artist.

The young man strolled along the riverbank with his brush, paint and canvas, looking for a beautiful scene to paint. Eventually, he found a wonderful spot. He immediately set up his canvas and tools and began working. When he finished, his painting appeared to be so real that one could almost feel the tickle of the grass underfoot and smell the wildflowers in bloom.

On his way home, the young man happened upon an old cottage that he desired to paint. He was so caught up in visualizing how the cottage would look on canvas that he accidentally tripped over a log and fell onto his art case, breaking his only paint brush. He was terribly distraught and began to cry out in despair.

There was a very **wise** old man who lived in the cottage who was disturbed by the **melee** and came outside to see what was wrong. After the boy calmed down, he told the man what had caused all the noise and confusion that had brought him outside. The man inspected the boy's painting and complimented him on his exceptional talent. He then told the boy that he had a magic paintbrush that brought pictures to life. The boy became very excited and begged the old man for the brush.

The man then revealed his true identity. He was an ancient magician named Marley. He told the youth that he would give him the brush on one condition—that he would paint a magnificent castle. Hastily, the boy drew the outline and painted the castle for Marley. When the boy finished, he took the painting from the stand and handed it to Marley, who was waiting with great anticipation. When Marley saw the picture, he became quite excited.

Since the boy had used the magic brush, the picture of the castle became a real castle. Marley quickly moved into his new home, but, before he left, he warned the boy to be careful when using the magic brush, because whatever he painted would come to life. The boy thanked him and ran home, excited and happy, with his new gift.

A year passed and the boy soon forgot Marley's warning. One day he painted a vicious, fire-breathing dragon. Before he could paint it away, the dragon picked up the boy to devour him. Marley suddenly appeared to rescue him and then confiscated the brush as punishment for not obeying his warning. In its place, however, he gave the young boy an authentic, professional paintbrush! The boy treasured his new gift and through hard work and dedication, eventually used it to become a famous artist.

Name ....

READING CHALLENGE

After reading "Marley the Magician," answer the following questions.

1. The short story is mainly about

2. Another word for melee is _____.

3. How did the boy break his only paintbrush?

4. Marley revealed his true identify, an ancient _____.

5. "The wise man who lived in the cottage, ..." In this sentence, wise means.

6. The magician gave the young boy the magic brush on one condition. What was the condition?

7. What happened to the boy when he painted a big, fire-breathing dragon?

8. Ceaselessly repeated or continuing without interruption are meanings of which bold-faced vocabulary word in the story?

9. What happened after the boy painted the magnificent castle for Marley the Magician?

Remember, if you don't know what a word means, look it up in a dictionary! You'll do better in the exercises!

Total Correct _____

Gentle Owners

My older sister had established a **precedent** in my family for odd first words uttered as an infant. We all know that the traditional "Ma-Ma," or "Da-Da," are the delightful words one first recognizes from the usual baby talk, but not for my sister! There just wasn't any mistaking her first spoken word. It was "e-a-t!" Then, she went on a little later to relay her first sentence: "Awnt eat out!" By the time I was born twelve years later, my parents were not at all surprised when, at the age of seven months, I came up with the word, "**Bu-et**."

What prompted my first word was an animal. On a Sunday afternoon before I was born, my father came home from a trip to Flagstaff, Arizona, accompanied by a rollicking, inexhaustibly excitable four-month-old bulldog pup he named "Bullet." Almost immediately, Bullet became the owner—lock, stock, and barrel—of our family. During his years with us, there was never any doubt in anybody's mind about who owned whom.

Bullet stormed into our family, took control of the premises and advised our gentle, old German shepherd, Yukon, and the cats, Autumn and Brandy, that from now on he would be in charge. He was white with copper spots and looked very **ominous**. However, Bullet had an engaging personality, wearing a perpetual grin, which, unfortunately, exposed all of his very dangerous-looking teeth.

Underneath this ferocious exterior beat a heart that was devoted to one thing—protecting his family. When I was born, Bullet decided that I was his primary responsibility. According to my mother, he would slip into the house, crawl under my crib, and proceed to lie there until she discovered and removed him. So, no one thought it too unusual that I came to bestow upon this sensitive, loving creature my first word, his name. Indeed, of all Bullet's daily chores, waiting for the mailman, meeting my sister's school bus and chasing strange dogs and cats out of the yard, his favorite was watching and protecting me as I grew up.

When I was about four years old, my father made another trip to the Flagstaff kennels. This time he came home with a funny-looking, female bulldog. My mother named her Huldy, a name she remembered from one of James Whitcomb Riley's poems. Immediately, Bullet became absolutely foolish over her, and the two soon became inseparable. Instead of hanging around with me in my playhouse under the walnut tree, Huldy and Bullet stayed down on the river bank searching for muskrat dens and chasing each other into the water.

I missed having Bullet around all the time, but it was great to see him having so much fun with his new friend!

READING CHALLENGE

After reading "Gentle Owners," fill in the correct answer bubble.

1. The story is mainly about
    - A. dogs are a great deal of trouble.
    - B. how important pets can be in a family.
    - C. pets should not be near young children.
    - D. dogs and cats can live together.

2. Bullet's daily chores consisted of all of the following things except
    - A. chasing strange dogs and cats.
    - B. waiting for the mailman.
    - C. protecting the family.
    - D. chasing rabbits and squirrels.

3. A word meaning an instance that can serve as an example in dealing with subsequent similar instances is
    - A. ominous.
    - B. precedent.
    - C. ferocious.
    - D. nonchalant.

4. Which dog's name came from one of James Whitcomb Riley's poems?
    - A. Bullet
    - B. Yukon
    - C. Huldy
    - D. Buford

5. <u>Ominous</u> means
    - A. cloudy.
    - B. threatening.
    - C. friendly.
    - D. steady.

6. How old was Bullet when he was brought home from Flagstaff?
    - A. 6 months
    - B. 2 years
    - C. 4 month
    - D. 4 years

Total Correct _____

Moonlit Night

The warm wind skids across the water
to reach my face.
The ropes attached to the boat creak
as they scrub across the posts.
The playful boats pat down on top of
the wavy water.
The wind seeps through the cracks of
the dock and causes a shrilling sound.
The snapping flag fights the wind
as best it can.
My hair surfs the waves of the wind.
The waves clash together like magnets.
The reflection of the moon covers
the water like a wet blanket.
The buoys in the water toss
around helplessly.
The pounding of footsteps echoes throughout
the dock and is carried
across the water by the wind as
I leave on this moonlit night.

Blue

Royal against the morn's dawn, light is
yet hindered by the mist.
Endangered by the **convening** clouds,
yet strong and valiant, it stands.
The sun struggles for resurrection,
as the clouds forbid its **intrusion**.
And I, bewildered, stand among the shadows,
as the rain pours down around me.

READING CHALLENGE

After reading both poems, circle the best answer for each question.

1. In "Blue," what is "Royal against the morn's dawn?"
   A. clouds
   B. mist
   C. rain
   D. light

2. What does the following line mean in "Moonlit Night?"
   "My hair surfs the waves of the wind."
   A. The poet is surfing on the ocean
   B. The wind is causing the hair to stand up
   C. The wind is violent and upsetting
   D. The water on the ocean is rising higher and higher

3. What is the subject of the following expression found in "Moonlit Night?"
   "The pounding of footsteps echoes throughout / the dock and is carried / across the water by the wind as / I leave on this moonlit night."
   A. footsteps
   B. echoes
   C. pounding
   D. block

4. "Endangered by the <u>convening</u> clouds, ..." **Convening** means
   A. assembling.
   B. disassembling.
   C. blackening.
   D. predictable.

5. "The snapping flag fights the wind / as best it can." What does this line mean?
   A. The wind overcomes the flag and it falls to the ground.
   B. The wind is blowing the flag fiercely, but the flag maintains.
   C. The flag is lightly waving in the air.
   D. The wind gently blows against the flag.

6. "The reflection of the moon covers / the water <u>like</u> a wet blanket." What is the literary device used in this expression?
   A. metaphor
   B. personification
   C. irony
   D. simile

7. A word that means the opposite of <u>intrusion</u> is
   A. force.
   B. evacuation.
   C. prowler.
   D. penetration.

8. In the poem "Blue," what does <u>its</u> represent in "The sun struggles for resurrections / as the clouds forbid <u>its</u> intrusion?"
   A. sun
   B. clouds
   C. resurrection
   D. intrusion

'LORIES

The sun rises early as the flowers slowly open to greet the new day. Of course, everyone knows that the first flower to bloom in the morning is the morning glory, and this morning Tracey is already outside picking them for her grandmother, who she calls Nana.

Today is Nana's birthday. Nana loves flowers, especially morning glories, so after filling her arms full of "lories," which is Tracey's nickname for morning glories, she hurries inside to grab a muffin from her mom before she races over to Nana's.

Tracey's mom has Tracey's bicycle waiting for her outside the back door. The bicycle is white, resplendent with daisies painted on it. She carefully lays her precious cargo in the little front basket and delicately places the still warm muffin into her pocket. Then off she goes, as fast as her feet can pedal!

Tracey never gets lost going to Nana's house for two reasons: 1. she follows the ruts through the yard, around the trees, and through the fence; and 2. she knows to turn right the minute that she hears the rushing sound of the waterfall. She never forgets to turn because the sound of the waterfall cascading from its colossal heights frightens her! When Tracey gets to Nana's fence, she notices that she has lost a few flowers, so she quickly runs to pick some more.

Tracey does not bother knocking before she barrels in because Nana always says, "Come right in" anyway. Nana is in the kitchen with her back turned to the door, preoccupied with rinsing cherries in the sink. Tracey tiptoes up behind her and yells, "Surprise!" at the top of her lungs. Nana jumps, "Baby Doll, you frightened me!" she shouts with a laugh. Of course, Nana knows Tracey was there. She just wants to make Tracey laugh.

Together they put the flowers in water and sit down to talk. Tracey pulls the muffin out from behind her back with a candle stuck on the top. She doesn't have any matches, but it doesn't matter. Nana pretends to blow out the candle anyway!

After they share the birthday muffin, they relax on the couch. Nana admires her flowers and says, "Tracey, I want you to always bring me morning glories just like you do now." Tracey promises she will. As the clock strikes eleven, Nana shouts, "Turn on the television! It's time for our show!"

Tracey quickly jumps up and turns on the television to their favorite game show. This is their favorite show because they like to guess the answers and pretend to "win" the prizes.

Tracey stays at Nana's house all day until her mother calls and tells her to come home. Before she goes, Tracey kisses Nana goodbye and then jumps on her bicycle. The next day, she returns to help Nana scrub and wash her porch. After they finish the **arduous** task, they decide to make homemade ice cream!

The ice cream maker is in the washroom, under some old clothes. The ice cream maker is a big wooden bucket with a crank on the outside and a smaller narrow bucket on the inside. Nana pulls the smaller bucket out. Then she mixes milk, sugar, eggs, vanilla flavoring, and peaches, pouring all of the ingredients into the container. Placing the lid back onto the smaller bucket, Nana then places it inside the big bucket. As Nana turns the crank, Tracey packs ice cubes around the small bucket.

After about twenty minutes, the ice cream is ready to eat. Tracey cannot believe how wonderful the ice cream tastes! Each of them has a big bowl, and the rest is put into the freezer for another day.

The next day Tracey does not visit Nana because it is Nana's day to play cards with her friends at the Senior Center. Tracey doesn't mind too much, but she does feel a little lonely. Late that afternoon, Nana calls to ask Tracey to spend the night with her. Tracey, of course, is **ecstatic**! They had the best time that night. They put on a fashion show with Nana's clothes and stayed up late to watch old movies.

It doesn't matter what they do. Tracey always has a great time with Nana! The next morning as Tracey wheeled her bicycle down the driveway, she turned to her grandmother who was standing on the porch and said, "Nana, when I grow up, I want to be just like you."

Name ....

READING CHALLENGE

After reading "Lories," answer the following questions.

Sequencing the Events

1. Number the sentences in the order in which they occurred in the story.

_____ Tracey tiptoes up behind her and yells, "Surprise!"

_____ They put on a fashion show with Nana's old clothes...

_____ ...Nana pretends to blow out the candle anyway

_____ ...they decide to make some homemade ice cream.

_____ She carefully lays her precious cargo in the little front basket.

_____ ...Tracey turns at the rushing sound of the waterfall.

Working with Vocabulary

Write the meaning for each word below.

2. ecstatic _____

3. arduous _____

Finding Details

4. What kind of show is Tracey's and Nana's favorite television show?

5. What is Nana's request of Tracey after she finishes her muffin?

6. What are 'lories?

7. When Tracey spends the night with Nana, what are two fun things they do?

Reading to Write

In a paragraph, discuss a family member that you are close to. What do you like to do together? What special memories do you share?

64   Total Correct _____

Lonely: An Essay

The smell of rotten garbage filled the frigid air as the old man rose from his snowy bed. His gray and silver hair was soiled and shaggy. His torn and tattered clothes were in similar repair. This was all that covered the lonely man inside. After all, when you feel like you have no purpose, it is easy to feel alone.

The garbage-strewn alley in which the man stood was dark except for a few cracks of light seeping out from under the locked doors of the tall, impersonal buildings. The walls were damp and covered with mildew. In the shadows of a doorway the lonely man could see a young boy and his family sleeping, exhausted from the relentless cold and their perpetual search for food. As he stared at the grim site before him, he thought about how much the boy reminded him of himself as a youth. His mind drifted back to a Christmas day remembering it as if it were just yesterday, even though forty years had passed.

He saw himself sitting by a festively decorated Christmas tree gazing into the dancing fire. He stretched his young limbs and ambled over to the tree to survey all the gifts. There was one box, long, skinny, and somewhat heavy, that particularly intrigued him. He shook the box until his mother told him to put it down. After she left the room, he snuck back over to the tree and shook the rest of the boxes until his arms began to ache. He was excited!

After checking all the presents, he went into the kitchen to watch his mother prepare Christmas dinner. The smell of sweet potatoes and turkey, cranberries and stuffing and luscious pies **wafted** through the air. He sat down at the table and began to daydream about all the great things that came with Christmas, including great presents. More than anything, he wanted a red bicycle. He was enthralled with the thought of riding it all around the neighborhood and racing all of his friends.

"Hey Jack! Let's go get something to eat," said the old man in the cardboard box next to him, snapping Jack back to his grim reality of today.

"Sure! In a minute," responded Jack, as he silently rose and wheeled his old red bicycle next to the boy's sleeping bag, who he had been watching.

"Everybody deserves to have their dreams come true," thought the lonely old man. A smile then spread across this face as he realized he wasn't quite as lonely anymore.

READING CHALLENGE

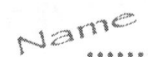

After reading "Lonely: An Essay," circle the best answer for each question.

1. **The essay is mainly about**
   A. decorating Christmas trees and exchanging Christmas gifts.
   B. a family forced to sleep on the streets.
   C. memories of a lonely, homeless man.
   D. the perfect Christmas dinner with all the trimmings.

2. **". . . pies wafted through the air." Wafted here means**
   A. moved forcibly through the air.
   B. moved gently through the air.
   C. baked at high temperatures.
   D. undisturbed in the air.

3. **In the essay, the old man is described with**
   A. shaggy, gray and silver hair.
   B. shaggy, gray and silver hair and green eyes.
   C. shaggy, gray and black hair.
   D. shaggy, gray and brown hair.

4. **What did the old man, as a young boy, want for Christmas?**
   A. motor bike and Daisy BB gun
   B. model airplane
   C. basketball
   D. big red bicycle

5. **"His mind drifted back to a Christmas day. . ."**
   A. twenty-four years past.
   B. four years past.
   C. fourteen years past.
   D. forty years past.

6. **What brings Jack back to reality?**
   A. the groaning of the young boy in the cardboard box next to him
   B. the yelling of a policeman as he was walking down the street
   C. an old man in the cardboard box next to him asking him to go get something to eat
   D. an old man rummaging through the garbage next to him

Total Correct _____

Good-bye Tomorrow

My family is like any other family in our small town of Ellisburg. We're not prestigious or flamboyant at all. In fact, I think we are a little bit boring.

This morning was just like any other around my house. Ellen and I were up at the crack of dawn beautifying ourselves while Mom was downstairs cooking breakfast and Dad was reading the morning paper.

"Okay, girls, breakfast is ready!" Mom yelled up from the bottom of the stairs. Yep, you're right. Just like an episode of some perfect family T.V. show!

Ellen and I dropped what we were doing, glanced at each other and took off running down the stairs like two greyhounds rounding the final turn on the race track.

The smell of bacon filled the air, making my taste buds beg for Mom's tasty cooking. Ellen and I piled our plates high with all the bacon, eggs, hash browns, and biscuits we could eat. Slowly we consumed the meal my mother had created. We took our time because this was our family meal. It was the only meal during the day when the four of us could sit down and eat together. Ellen and I were at school for lunch, and during dinner, it seemed as if something was always **infiltrating** our quality family time, whether it was school meetings, my mom's aerobics classes or Dad's business meeting. Still, breakfast was a meal and a time we could always count on being together.

This Friday morning was like all other mornings in that each of us ate while we discussed the latest activities, news and gossip around town. Our topic of conversation suddenly took a peculiar turn when Dad began quizzing Ellen.

"Ellen, are you going out with Ted tonight?" my dad asked.

"No!" she blurted. "We're never going out again!" Then she ran out the door to school.

Ted and my sister had been dating forever. They were always together and because they were both patient and talkative about their feelings, they rarely fought. A few months ago, Ted had even given Ellen a promise ring even though both were planning to attend different universities in the fall. Until last night, Ellen had been on top of the world. But now something changed. I knew that recently they had been talking about the upcoming fall and spending time apart. The talk was difficult and each felt angry and afraid that this was the end of their relationship. They hadn't been able to resolve their feelings and they both felt terrible.

Usually, since Ellen and I were more like best friends than actual sisters, she would tell me about their arguments and disagreements as soon as he walked out the door. But Ellen never told me about this one—I overheard it. That night, after we got home from school, I watched Ellen go into her room shutting the door behind her. I could hear her crying.

Good-bye Tomorrow, continued

I finally couldn't wait any longer and I went in. Standing over her bed I asked her, "What's up?" She was silent so I asked her again. She still did not answer. "Are you okay?" I asked.

"Sure," was her reply. An **eerie** silence filled the air and after a few minutes slowly passed, she continued, "I'm fine. In fact, I've never been better. How about you?"

"Actually," I said, "I'm feeling slightly left out. I wish you would talk to me."

Ellen stood up and as she walked across the room she mumbled, "Trust me, you're better off not knowing." She stopped by the window and stood staring into the distance. When she heard me stand, she said, "On your way out, could you shut the door, please?" Knowing that trying to pressure her would accomplish nothing, I did as she requested and left her alone.

The week was very difficult for her. Everyday was the same routine: she went to school, came home, did homework, and went to bed. Everyone knew something was wrong, but she would talk to no one. She rarely spoke a word and when she did, it was always only a few short sentences. I tried daily to make her talk about what had happened between Ted and her, but she never even gave me a clue about why they were arguing.

"Ellen, what are you doing tonight?" my dad asked her a few nights later.

I glanced at Ellen and feeling my eyes on her, she sprang out of her seat, looked at my father, and said, "I'm not doing anything tonight!"

"You're not?" my dad questioned. "What is going on honey? What is the matter with you and Ted."

"I told you, it's over with Ted!" she said as she stormed out the door.

I could not concentrate at all during school the next day. I was so anxious to get home that afternoon, hoping that Ellen and I would be home alone. I was planning to make her talk!

When I finally did arrive home, Ellen was waiting for me. I could tell she was calmer and felt like talking. She explained that she and Ted had decided they would follow their dreams of going away to the schools they chose. They felt it would be difficult to date, but both wanted to remain close friends. At first they were angry and afraid of losing each other. Each wished things could be different. Then Ellen described how she had thought things out at school that day and had come to some conclusions. Ted was still worried, but she assured him that their decision would work for the best.

"I now realize that going away will be good for both of us," Ellen said. "We can use this time apart as a chance to learn and grow. I feel a lot better now. I am strong."

Ellen talked to Mom and Dad later that night. I saw a lot more of my sister after that and I liked it. After all, she is one of my best friends even if we are normal!

READING CHALLENGE

After reading "Good-bye Tomorrow," answer the following questions.

1. The story is mainly about

2. Number the sentences in the order in which they occurred in the story.
   _____ Ted and my sister had been dating forever.
   _____ Ellen talked to Mom and Dad later that night.
   _____ She stopped by the window and stood staring into the distance.
   _____ When I finally did arrive home, Ellen was waiting for me.
   _____ My family is like any other family.
   _____ "Ellen are you going out with Ted tonight?"

3. Ellen's family was like any other family in Ellisburg because
   A. the narrator was the most popular girl in the eighth grade.
   B. Ellen was the senior class beauty.
   C. they were not prestigious or flamboyant.
   D. Ellen and the narrator made good grades at school.

4. One of the words listed below that means <u>esteemed</u> is
   A. infiltrated.
   B. distracted.
   C. devastated.
   D. prestigious.

5. A word that means <u>to draw away from something</u> is
   A. eerie.
   B. distracted.
   C. infiltrated.
   D. blundered.

6. What vocabulary word means <u>weird or mysterious</u>?

7. During what part of the day was the family always together?

8. Why did Ellen and Ted decide to stop dating, but remain friends?

9. Discuss an emotional pain that you have had and how you dealt with it.

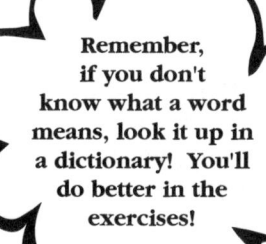

Remember, if you don't know what a word means, look it up in a dictionary! You'll do better in the exercises!

Total Correct _____

The Coldest Place on Earth

If one goes to the southernmost part of the Earth, he or she will arrive at the continent of Antarctica. This **desolate** continent covers over 5,000,000 square miles and is almost entirely covered by an ice cap. This ice cap is over two miles thick in some places. About 90% of the world's ice is located there, and the coldest recorded temperatures on Earth are found on this continent. In 1960, a temperature of −127° F was recorded!

During the cold southern winters, ice accumulates in the Antarctic region and reaches as far north as the 60th parallel. A drifting sheet of ice several hundred miles wide, called an ice belt, surrounds Antarctica and makes the mainland difficult to reach by ship. Only during the short summer season, December and January, is it possible for icebreaker ships to cut through the ice and get to the interior regions of the continent.

Unlike the northern Arctic region, Antarctica has no native human life. The few people who actually live there arrived as recently as 1957 from other countries. They live at scientific research stations that have been set up in various locations. The work carried out at these stations is for the purpose of gaining a better understanding of the earth and the atmosphere that surrounds it. The United States, Russia, Great Britain, France and Australia are only a few of the countries that have been active in Antarctica. They have set up research stations there in geology, **glaciology**, biology, and meteorology.

Many countries claimed portions of the continent as their own but in 1959, the twelve nations that have been active in this area signed a treaty in which they agreed to delay the settlement of any claims for thirty years. Most importantly, it was agreed that the continent of Antarctica should be used for peaceful purposes only, which means that no nuclear testing or other such experiments can be carried out there.

READING CHALLENGE

After reading "The Coldest Place on Earth," answer the following questions.

1. The vocabulary word that means "the study of glaciers" is _____.

2. The coldest recorded temperature in Antarctica was _____.

3. Name at least five countries that have set up research stations in Antarctica.

4. When is the short summer season in Antarctica?

5. The continent of Antarctica covers how much area?

6. An antonym for a word that means "having few or no inhabitants" is _____.

7. What percent of the world's ice is found in Antarctica?

Total Correct _____

Colors of Christmas

Sitting in front of the fire by the **glittering** Christmas tree, I watched my four-year-old daughter, Jill, intently coloring page after page in her coloring book. As I watched her, I remembered how I used to love to color. I would sit in my grandmother's lap and color until my mother called me to help in the kitchen or do some other chore. Then my grandmother would gently say, "Mandy, your mother is calling. You run along and help, and I'll wait right here for you." Reluctantly, I would leave my grandmother until I had completed whatever tasks my mother had assigned me. After I was finished, I would race back to my coloring book and continue wherever I had left off.

Close to Christmas one year, Grandmother visited Aunt Agnes, who lived up North. Every day while she was gone, I would sit in her old wooden rocking chair and color a picture for her. She loved my pictures, and I wanted to give her my best.

The day before Christmas there was a knock at the door. When Mother opened it, a man in a gray uniform was standing on our front porch holding a package. The package was wrapped in brown paper and tied with a red string. After reading the name on the package, Mother handed it to me, saying, "This is for you." I opened the card and read what it said: "Merry Christmas. I miss you. With love, Grandmother." Excitement **pulsated** through my veins, I ripped open the box and found a brand new coloring book and a new set of crayons!

Suddenly a tug on my sleeve and a voice at my side brought me back to reality. "Mommy! Mommy! Will you help me color?" I gently pulled my precious daughter onto my lap and hugged her tightly, thinking that the colors of Christmas had never been so beautiful.

READING CHALLENGE

After reading "Colors of Christmas," circle the best answer for each question.

1. **"Colors of Christmas," is mainly about**
   A. memories of past Christmases.
   B. memories of doing chores.
   C. memories of baking cakes.
   D. memories of learning to sew.

2. **Pulsating means**
   A. to vibrate or quiver.
   B. to waste or dispose of.
   C. to be sad.
   D. to be free.

3. **Who is the narrator?**
   A. Grandmother
   B. Jill
   C. Aunt Agnes
   D. Mandy

4. **Glittering means**
   A. to shine brightly.
   B. shining with a dim light.
   C. spell-binding effect.
   D. examining an area.

5. **Write about something that you enjoy doing now, that you think your children will enjoy doing.**

Remember, if you don't know what a word means, look it up in a dictionary! You'll do better in the exercises!

Total Correct _____

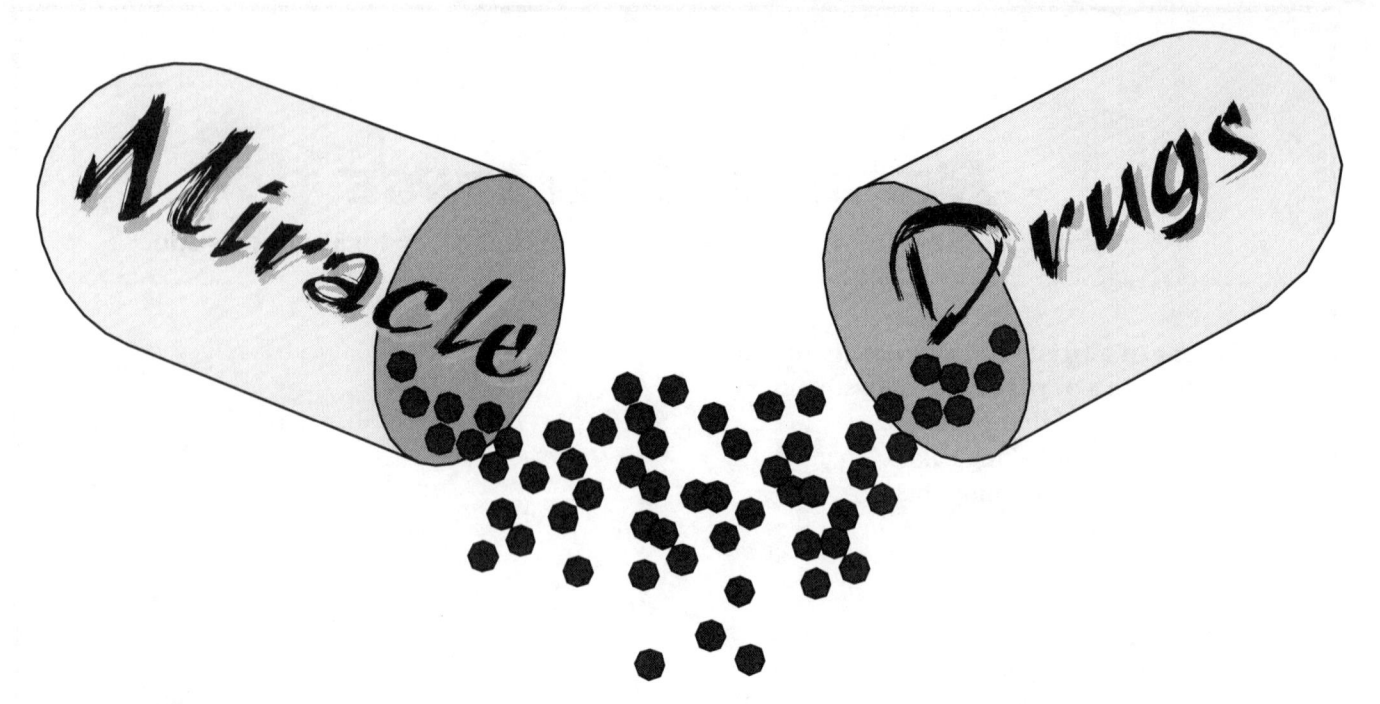

Miracle Drugs

Pulling on his ears and **wrenching** his head from side to side, the baby is fretful and warm. Her heart **wreathed** with fear, the young mother telephones the doctor. The receptionist calmly tells the mother to bring the infant into the office. When they arrive, the mother is told to take her son into the examination room. Dr. Sanders is waiting. The doctor checks the baby's temperature, throat, and ears. Then Dr. Sanders tells the mother that her child has a mild ear infection and that with antibiotics, he should **recuperate** in about a week.

Have you ever wondered what those miracle antibiotics really are? Anti means "against" and biotic means "life." However, antibiotics only wage war against microscopic forms of life called "bacteria," which cause disease. Sometimes these diseases are relatively mild, like a baby's earache, but sometimes they can be **fatal**.

Sir Alexander Fleming pioneered the search for effective medicines against disease beginning with his discovery of penicillin in 1928. Other scientists scoured the world for soil samples that might contain the types of molds that produce antibiotics. These life-giving medicines are derived from living matter, such as bacteria, plants, and molds.

No one is exactly certain how antibiotics **inhibit** the growth of bacteria. What we do know is that certain antibiotics are effective against certain bacteria, but not necessarily against others. This is why doctors tell their patients to take all the prescribed medication and throw away any unused pills. Some people are allergic to some or all antibiotics.

On the whole, antibiotics have drastically reduced the incidence of death or serious illness from disease or infection since their discovery. Antibiotics are indeed miracle drugs.

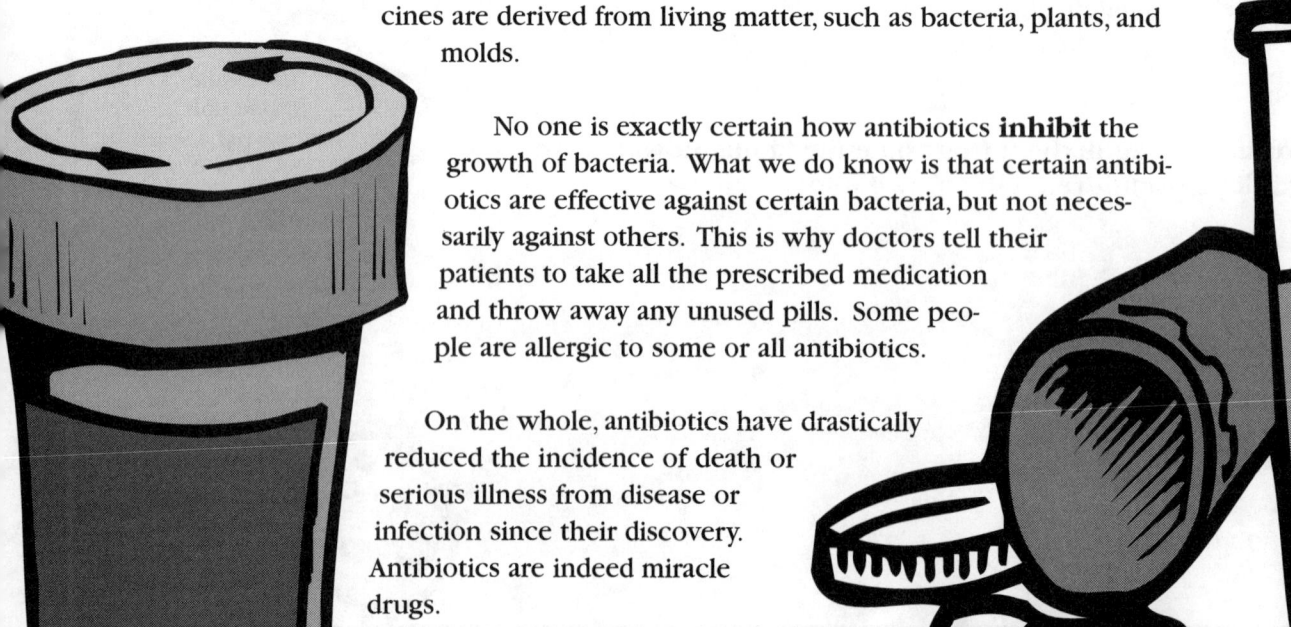

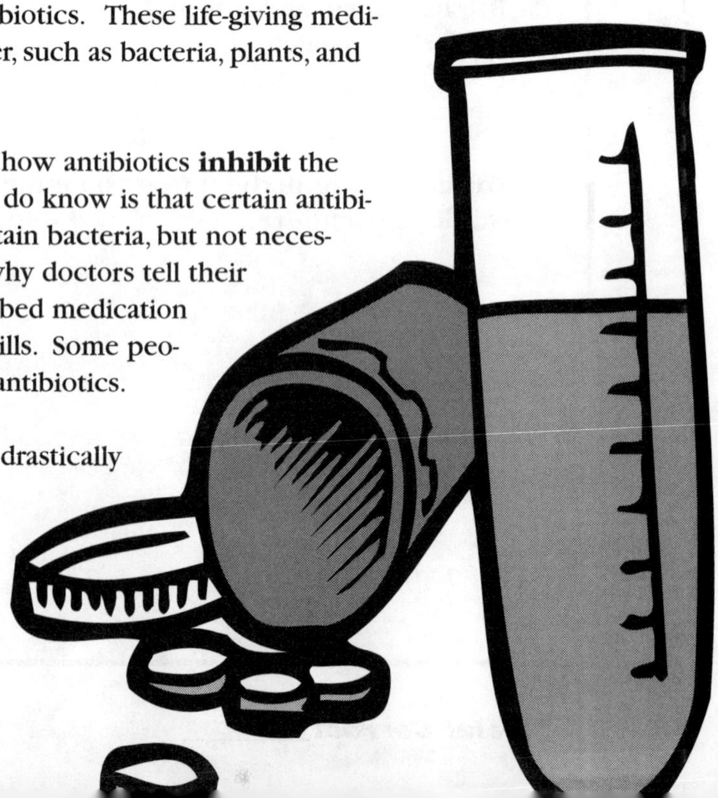

Name ....

READING CHALLENGE

After reading "Miracle Drugs," answer the following questions.

1. What are "miracle drugs?"

2. Who discovered penicillin and when?

3. What do "anti" and "biotic" mean?

4. The word that means <u>to entwine, twist or surround</u> is _____.

5. Antibiotics are derived from such living matter as _____.

6. Which one of the words listed below means <u>capable of causing death</u>?

      inhibit   wrenching   recuperate   fatal

Total Correct _____

In My Dreams

In my dreams there is a place where all my toys can come alive,
a magical place, a mythical place, where spirits do readily revive.

The clowns stop juggling and begin to dance; carousel horses joke instead of prance.
And Pooh Bear sets down his honey pot to see what Piglet and Tigger got.

Raggedy Ann relaxes her smile, but only for a little while.
Andy even tries a frown. Even smiling has its ups and downs.

Crybaby giggles in little spurts, then laughs and laughs until she hurts.
Then just before the morning sun, there's pretend tea for everyone.

Then they retire to where they were,
no longer **discontented**, bored or spurred.

Reading Challenge

After reading "In My Dreams," fill in the correct answer bubble.

1. "In My Dreams," is mainly about
   - A. taking care of toys and learning responsibility.
   - B. living on a farm with all kinds of animals.
   - C. baby-sitting younger siblings when parents go out for the night.
   - D. escaping the real world into a make-believe world.

2. ". . .no longer discontented, bored, or spurred." <u>Discontented</u> means
   - A. feeling tired and sleepy.
   - B. unhappy or dissatisfied.
   - C. being satisfied and content.
   - D. angry and afraid.

3. ". . . carousel horses joke instead of prance." Since horses do not "joke," what is the literary device used in this expression?
   - A. simile
   - B. pun
   - C. personification
   - D. metaphor

Ice Cream Memories

When I awoke that morning, I knew I should have played sick or something. It was the day set aside for our family reunion, and soon I would be crowded in between cousins so distant that I had never even met them. There would be old people sitting around talking about times long before I was even born. I had dreaded this day all year long, and now there was no way to avoid it.

When we arrived at a tiny white house belonging to my grandparents, there were uncles lounging on the front porch while aunts were hurrying about in the kitchen. Some of my cousins were already there, running around and playing games. I gave a long, sad look at my mother who returned the same with a less than sympathetic glance.

As we went inside, I was smothered with hugs and kisses, even by people I hardly knew or had never met before. Retreating to the living room where I knew Grandpa would be, I had barely walked through the door when he burst into laughter. He was laughing at all the different shades of lipstick on my face, together with my **solemn** and uncaring attitude.

"Kate, you look worse than your grandma," my Grandpa said, as he motioned for me to come closer so that he could give me a big hug. Grandpa was never one to beat around the bush. He always spoke his mind. "Let's get out of here," he said to me with a grin. I did not argue.

We **sauntered** downtown to the drugstore, which was only a few blocks from where my grandparents lived. Normally, it would only take about ten minutes to walk the distance, but today it took nearly twenty minutes to walk. Neither one of us was in a hurry. The town drugstore was a hangout for the senior citizens who would go there to eat ice cream and tell stories.

Grandpa bought us ice cream and then we sat down and he began to talk. Somehow, my grandpa always understood me, more, sometimes, than my own parents. He knew I would rather be with him than with any of my cousins at the reunion. Furthermore, Grandpa knew I enjoyed his stories, even when he told the same ones over and over again.

77

Ice Cream Memories
continued

When we could **tarry** no longer, we walked back to Grandpa's house, and stopped by the grocery store to pick up some more ice cream for later. This was our excuse for leaving. It didn't cross our minds that we had been gone for an hour. Since it was still relatively early in the day, not many people missed us. Anyway, Grandpa and I had followed this routine for as long as I could remember.

Grandpa always called me "Kate," but my real name is Elizabeth. I do not think he even knew my real name. My parents did not like him calling me Kate because they were afraid I would be confused later in life. However, I was not worried. I did not see anything weird about it.

My grandpa and I agreed about everything. We both liked to eat desserts, watch a good football game, and help people in need. Sometimes, our relatives felt excluded because of our special friendship, but we never intentionally left anyone out.

As they always do, the years flew by. I became caught up in school and my friends. I visited Grandpa less and less. I would call sometimes, but suddenly it had been years since Grandpa and I had gone for ice cream. Finally, one day in my senior year in high school, I decided to drive over to Grandpa's.

It was a pleasant drive, winding along shaded, suburban streets. When I arrived, it did not take us very long to pick up where we had left off. There was always that special bond between us which kept us together even when we were apart.

That day we would make our final walk together to the drugstore for ice cream cones. I noticed that many of Grandpa's friends were not there anymore, but his stories were just as **intriguing** and interesting. When I drove away that afternoon, he was grinning from ear to ear, and that's how I will remember him for the rest of my life.

READING CHALLENGE

After reading "Ice Cream Memories," circle the best answer for each question.

1. The story is mainly about
    A. eating ice cream at the drugstore.
    B. cherishing memories of grandparents.
    C. family reunions.
    D. friends at school.

2. We sauntered downtown to the drugstore. Sauntered means
    A. strolled leisurely.
    B. hurried quickly.
    C. drove slowly.
    D. jogged swiftly.

3. What happened last?
    A. Grandpa bought us ice cream.
    B. I would call Grandpa sometimes.
    C. When I drove away that afternoon, Grandpa was grinning from ear to ear.
    D. He began laughing again so hard that I had to whack him on the back.

4. Intriguing means
    A. repulsing.
    B. intimidating.
    C. fascinating.
    D. boring.

5. Grandpa and Kate agreed about everything except
    A. helping people when they are in need.
    B. watching a good football game.
    C. eating desserts.
    D. their favorite pizza.

6. How does Kate feel about attending the reunion?
    A. eager to see her cousins
    B. dreaded this day
    C. looked forward to eating good food
    D. looked forward to meeting new relatives

7. In this selection, tarry means
    A. to speak.
    B. to delay or be late.
    C. to eat.
    D. to run.

8. Why is the story called, "Ice Cream Memories?"
    A. because ice cream was the main dessert at the reunion
    B. because ice cream was always on sale at the grocery store
    C. because Kate and Grandpa ate ice cream when they visited
    D. because Grandpa knew how to make the best peach ice cream

9. In the story, solemn means
    A. deeply serious.
    B. frivolous.
    C. informal.
    D. light.

10. Kate was in what year of school when she last visited grandpa?
    A. 6th grade
    B. 4th grade
    C. 8th grade
    D. 12th grade

Total Correct _____

BABY'S FIRST THOUGHTS

I opened my eyes and saw a woman sitting there smiling, crying, and gazing at me at the same time. My eyes began to search the room and came to rest on a man with a single tear rolling down his cheek.

I was trying to **ascertain** why the man and woman were crying, but I just could not comprehend. As I examined these people more closely, my gaze fell on another man who looked absolutely hilarious dressed in a large gown with small blue dots. "These are definitely some strange people," I thought.

Suddenly, I felt a pair of warm hands lifting me into the air. The face of the person lifting me was very neat and orderly looking, and she said, "Mr. and Mrs. Williamson, I'm going to take little Stacey into the nursery. I'm sure you're very tired and need some rest."

She then carried me into a room filled with other babies. Glancing at the baby beside me, I noticed he looked rather funny. He was bald! I felt my own head and discovered to my **dismay** that I was too. I thought, "Oh no, this is so devastating! I can't go through life with no hair!"

My eyelids felt very heavy, and I drifted off to sleep. Later, I awoke to a woman hovering over me. "Are you hungry? Do you want a bottle?" Without giving me a chance to answer, she stuck something soft and rubbery in my mouth.

The next day was much the same, with two exceptions. The woman and man I had first seen were beginning to look somewhat better. Furthermore, I had been sleeping a great deal lately, but today when I awoke, I was in a much larger and softer bed. "Ah, what a relief!" I thought as I stretched out.

I felt that I was being watched, so I turned my head, and a big kid chuckled and exclaimed, "Mommy! Mommy! She's awake!"

I studied the kid closely, and saw that he had hair. "No fair!" I thought, envying his curly blonde locks. Continuing to gaze at his silly face, I noticed someone familiar coming toward me. That kid said "Mommy" and she responded. I would have to remember that the next time I wanted something!

When the woman came very close to me, she whispered, "Lee, don't scream." I assumed she was speaking to that kid because I had not said a word, but she then rubbed her hand over my bald head. Finally, the two of them went away leaving me to stare at the ceiling.

Feeling alone, I cried out for the woman to come back. She came back, picked me up and started whispering, "I love you, Stacey."

I think I'm going to like this "Mommy," very much.

READING CHALLENGE

After reading "Baby's First Thoughts," circle the best answer for each question.

1. **Who is telling the story?**
   A. Mr. Williamson
   B. Mrs. Williamson
   C. nurse
   D. baby

2. **The baby observed the following except**
   A. its bald head.
   B. someone say "Mommy."
   C. a gown with small blue dots.
   D. the plaid wallpaper around the room.

3. **In the selection, dismay means**
   A. satisfaction.
   B. contentment.
   C. fear.
   D. happiness.

4. **What happened first?**
   A. Stacey opened her eyes and saw . . . .
   B. Stacey studied the little kid closely.
   C. Stacey felt a pair of warm hands.
   D. Stacey's words sounded like a cry.

5. **In the story, ascertain means**
   A. to suppose.
   B. to find out.
   C. to guess.
   D. to feel.

6. **Where is the setting of the story?**
   A. parent's house
   B. kindergarten
   C. hospital and home
   D. grandparents' house

7. **In the phrase, "I was trying to ascertain why the man and woman were crying . . . ." Who are the man and woman?**
   A. mother and father
   B. doctor and nurse
   C. mother and doctor
   D. nurse and Lee

Remember, if you don't know what a word means, look it up in a dictionary! You'll do better in the exercises!

Total Correct _____

Mariah Carey

Mariah Carey was born on March 27, 1970, in Long Island, New York. Her mother was an Irish opera singer from Indiana, and her father was a Venezuelan **aeronautical** engineer. Mariah was the third child in her family. She has an older sister, Allison, and an older brother, Morgan.

At the age of two, Mariah demonstrated her developing talent for the first time. Her mother, Patricia, was rehearsing Verdi's *Rigoletto* when she missed a cue. Mariah sang it perfectly from the right spot. Patricia was surprised and pleased with Mariah's gift and began giving her singing lessons.

Mariah's parents divorced when she was three years old. Mariah and Morgan stayed with their mother, and Allison went with her father.

By the time she graduated from high school, Mariah had been introduced to Ben Margulies, who owned a recording studio. With his help, Mariah wrote some of her early songs. At age eighteen, Mariah became a backup singer for Brenda Starr. She toured with Starr for about a year. Then, in 1988 Starr introduced Mariah to some people from CBS Records. They were impressed with her voice and offered Mariah a recording contract.

By March, 1992, Mariah had made two hit CD's and made her first live appearance on MTV's "Unplugged." Mariah has won numerous awards, including *Best New Artist*, *Best Pop Vocal Female*, three *Soul Train* awards, and many more. Mariah Carey has touched the lives of many people throughout the world with her beautiful voice and lyrics.

READING CHALLENGE

After reading "Mariah Carey," fill in the correct answer bubble.

1. Which happened first?
   - A. Mariah has won numerous awards, including Best New Artist....
   - B. At age eighteen Mariah became a backup singer for Brenda Starr
   - C. Mariah was the third child in her family....
   - D. This occurred when Patricia, her mother, was rehearsing Verdi's *Rigoletto*

2. At age eighteen, Mariah
   - A. demonstrated her extraordinary talent for the first time.
   - B. toured with Brenda Starr for about a year.
   - C. met some people from RCA Records.
   - D. had already made two hit CD's.

3. How old was Mariah when her parents divorced?
   - A. two years old
   - B. eighteen years old
   - C. twenty-one years old
   - D. three years old

4. From what country does Mariah's father come?
   - A. Venezuela
   - B. America
   - C. Brazil
   - D. France

5. <u>Aeronautical</u> means
   - A. of or relating to building houses.
   - B. of or relating to aircraft.
   - C. of or relating to ships.
   - D. of or relating to trains.

6. Mariah was offered a recording contract by
   - A. NBC Television.
   - B. CBS Records.
   - C. Los Anglos Lakers.
   - D. Time Warner.

Total Correct _____

The Growing Process

There was a tree whose limbs were bare.
Then the sun came out and tiny blossoms were there.
They were so small in the beginning—nearly naked to the eye.
But soon they started to grow—
Thanks to the sun high in the sky.

The tree grew and grew until it was as full as it could be.
All through the summer it was a <u>shrouded</u> place for me.
When summer grew to a close, I left it alone.
Then, I came home from school one day.
My tree, I discovered, had changed in a distinct way.

Its leaves were dressed in scarlet and gold.
The seasons had changed, or so I was told.
I was young and did not know all.
My tree had suddenly changed. The leaves began to fall.
"It just isn't fair." I wanted to call.

Soon the leaves will all be gone.
Mother tried to explain as best she could.
She said he'd be back—she promised he would.
She said he had grown tired and had to rest.
It was all part of his growing process.

Tulips

The scarlet tulips rise from the green forest floor,
hoping to find the sunlight they richly adore.

The golden light showers them with sunburst crystals,
as their <u>ebony</u> centers reach out to capture it.

When the day is over and the <u>crimson</u> petals close,
They will pursue the light another day.

READING CHALLENGE

After reading both poems, circle the best answer for each question.

1. Another word for shrouded in "The Growing Process" is
   A. concealed.
   B. uncovered.
   C. happy.
   D. busy.

2. In the fourth stanza, what is the antecedent for he?

   ". . . she promised he would."

   A. narrator
   B. father
   C. tree
   D. blossom

3. What is the "golden light," in "Withering Tulips?"
   A. scarlet tulips
   B. sun
   C. forest floor
   D. crystals

4. In "Withering Tulips," the word crimson means
   A. black.
   B. orange.
   C. purple.
   D. red.

5. In the first stanza of "The Growing Process," which two end words rhyme?
   A. eye — there
   B. there — grow
   C. bare — eye
   D. eye — sky

6. In "The Growing Process," where does the narrator spend the summer?
   A. in the tree
   B. at school
   C. in the scarlet tulips
   D. with the mother

7. " . . . as their ebony centers reach out to capture it." In "Withering Tulips," ebony means
   A. red.
   B. black.
   C. scarlet.
   D. purple.

8. Why had the tree changed?
   A. It was pouting
   B. It was fall
   C. It needed fertilizer
   D. It didn't like summer

9. In "The Growing Process," which writing technique is used in the following line: "She said he had grown tired and had to rest?"
   A. simile
   B. metaphor
   C. personification
   D. pun

Total Correct _____   85

Gypsies

The Gypsies, a distinct ethnic group that originated in Northern Central India, are a wandering people.

They were first known as the "Dom," in India. They were seen as a low caste and earned their living singing and dancing. The Dom began migrating from India in the ninth century. As they migrated through the Middle East, the "D," of Dom was replaced by an "R." The Gypsies today refer to themselves as the "Rom," meaning "man." Today there are an estimated eight to ten million Gypsies in more than forty countries, an estimated one million of them in North America. The Gypsies are found all over the world, in the country and in the cities. Their customs have remained unchanged for centuries.

Throughout history, Gypsies have been considered a mysterious group. Their belief in magic frightens some people and their unwillingness to **assimilate** into Christian culture has resulted in **persecution**. In the Middle Ages they, like the Jews, were accused of bringing plagues into Europe.

In the nineteenth and twentieth centuries, the Gypsies suffered many further injuries and they were specifically victimized by the Nazi Germans during World War II. Gypsies faced continued persecution in European Communist societies. In the USSR, during Nikita Khrushchev's premiership, Gypsies led a settled life. With the collapse of Eastern European Communism in 1989, renewed ethnic violence victimized the Gypsies as well as other minorities.

Most of the Gypsies living in the United States today are descended from immigrants of Eastern Europe during the 1880's, 1890's and 1900's. The Gypsies of North America, as well as those of Europe, live and work in extended family groups, known as kumpania. Whenever possible, they resist working as wage laborers because they prefer to be self-employed. Many women still practice the art of fortune telling, usually by using **palmistry**.

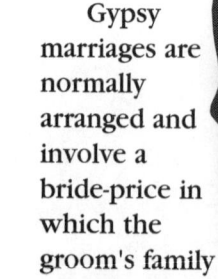

Gypsy marriages are normally arranged and involve a bride-price in which the groom's family must pay a large sum to the bride's family. In North America, the bride customarily joins the groom's household in a special arrangement.

Reading Challenge

After reading "Gypsies," fill in the correct answer bubble.

1. What is another word for <u>assimilate</u>?
    - A. reject
    - B. unwilling
    - C. incorporate
    - D. persecute

2. Gypsies today refer to themselves as
    - A. Rom, meaning "man."
    - B. Rom, meaning "woman."
    - C. Dom, meaning "man."
    - D. Dom, meaning "woman."

3. Most of the Gypsies living in the U.S. today are descended from immigrants of
    - A. Western Europe.
    - B. Southern Europe.
    - C. Northern Europe.
    - D. Eastern Europe.

4. Many women still practice the art of
    - A. seamstress.
    - B. selling used cars.
    - C. fortune telling.
    - D. housekeeper.

5. A word meaning "the state of being oppressed or harassed," is
    - A. assimilate.
    - B. persecution.
    - C. nomadic.
    - D. mystical.

6. Gypsies originated in
    - A. Germany.
    - B. India.
    - C. USSR.
    - D. North America.

7. One reason the Gypsies were persecuted was
    - A. controlled too much land.
    - B. a strong belief in Christianity.
    - C. unwillingness to assimilate into Christian Culture.
    - D. an alliance with the Jews.

8. How many Gypsies are estimated to be living in North America today?
    - A. eight million
    - B. ten million
    - C. one million
    - D. forty million

9. <u>Palmistry</u> means
    - A. practice of telling fortunes, using the palms of the hand.
    - B. predicting the weather, using the palms of the hand.
    - C. communicating with others, using the palms of hands.
    - D. using the palms of the hands to create sounds.

Total Correct _____

Hillary Rodham Clinton

Hillary Rodham Clinton, born in Park Ridge, Illinois, on October 26, 1947, is the wife of President William Jefferson Clinton. As a young girl, Hillary participated in many activities, including Girl Scouts, swimming, tennis, ballet, softball, skating, and field hockey. She was active in student government and enjoyed taking debate classes where she learned the value of looking at issues from more than one point of view. Hillary considered many careers, including becoming an astronaut. Eventually, she decided to become a lawyer.

An early influence in Hillary's life was the minister of her church, who taught her the importance of being involved in her community. She took his teachings very seriously and began tutoring children and organizing food drives. With her church youth group, she helped raise money to care for less fortunate children.

She attended Wellesley College, in Wellesley, Massachusetts, where she was president of the student government. After graduating in 1969, she attended Yale Law School, where she met fellow student Bill Clinton. Both received their law degrees in 1973. During the summer of 1974, she worked with the Judiciary Committee of the U.S. House of Representatives.

Hillary Rodham married Bill Clinton on November 11, 1975. Hillary practiced law with a Little Rock firm and eventually became a partner. After Bill Clinton's **inauguration**, as governor of Arkansas on January 10, 1979, she was appointed head of the state's Rural Health Advisory Committee, which tried to improve rural health care. She was named *Arkansas Woman of the Year*, *Arkansas Young Mother of the Year*, and was twice named one of the *Most Influential Lawyers in America* by the National Law Journal. During her Arkansas years, Hillary Rodham Clinton served on the boards of several corporations, including Wal-Mart. She gave up those positions when her husband began his presidential campaign.

When Bill Clinton became President of the United States in 1992, Hillary quickly began her work as First Lady. She wanted to make the White House a true home for her husband and daughter, Chelsea. She **converted** the serving kitchen on the second floor into an informal family kitchen so that they could sit down together for meals just as they had done in Arkansas. Taking on a political role, she also became the chief of a White House task force on national health care reform, where she worked as an unpaid volunteer.

As First Lady, Mrs. Clinton travels throughout this country and around the world. She enjoys meeting young people and sharing with them the President's and her belief that with everyone's help, we can make our country a better place for all Americans.

READING CHALLENGE

After reading "Hillary Rodham Clinton," circle the best answer for each question.

1. Another word for <u>converted</u> is
   A. stable.
   B. changed.
   C. judiciary.
   D. inauguration.

2. As a young girl, Hillary participated in
   A. tennis, ballet, softball, volleyball.
   B. tennis, ballet, baseball, skating.
   C. tennis, ballet, softball, skating.
   D. tennis, softball, skating, sewing.

3. Hillary was born in
   A. Little Rock.
   B. Washington, D.C..
   C. Oak Ridge.
   D. Park Ridge.

4. In college, Hillary was
   A. president of student government.
   B. president of the debate team.
   C. president of the law club.
   D. secretary of student government.

5. The Clintons' daughter's name is
   A. Billie.
   B. Rodham.
   C. Chelsea.
   D. Wellesley.

6. Hillary was born on
   A. January 10, 1977.
   B. October 26, 1947.
   C. November 11, 1945.
   D. October 26, 1943.

7. <u>Inauguration</u> means
   A. a formal wedding honoring two people.
   B. a formal reception.
   C. an informal ceremony.
   D. a formal ceremony installing a person in a position.

8. Hillary Rodham Clinton received all of the following awards except
   A. *Arkansas Woman of the Seventies.*
   B. *Arkansas Woman of the Year.*
   C. *Most Influential Lawyer in America.*
   D. *Arkansas Young Mother of the Year.*

9. Where did Hillary receive her law degree?
   A. Wellesley
   B. Yale
   C. Little Rock
   D. Princeton

Total Correct _____

Charleston

Charleston is South Carolina's oldest city and the second largest city in the state. With well preserved homes and buildings from the 1700's and 1800's, Charleston also has some of the country's oldest landscaped gardens.

Named for King Charles II of England, the city was originally called Charles Towne until its present name was adopted in 1783. Charleston, founded by English and British West Indies settlers in 1670, was the birthplace of the Confederacy in 1861. The city was the state capital until 1790 when the seat of government was moved to Columbia.

Charleston has a mild climate with an average annual temperature of 65°F. It has humid summers and mild winters.

There are many historical sights to see in Charleston. Among them are: the Hunley Museum, Cypress Gardens, Yorktown Carrier, Magnolia Plantation, Edmonston-Alston House and Heyward-Washington House. Other points of interest include The Citadel (a military college), the College of Charleston, the Medical University, and the Spoleto Festival U.S.A.

Charleston has a **diversified** industry. Its manufactured goods include paper, fertilizers, textiles, and chemicals. Furthermore, it is the site of a U.S. Naval Base and Charleston Air Force Base, which is part of the Military Airlift Command.

The city is **vulnerable** to earthquakes and hurricanes. In 1886, the city was struck by one of the most severe earthquakes ever to occur in the eastern U.S. Also, in 1989 Hurricane Hugo badly damaged Charleston and its surrounding area.

READING CHALLENGE

After reading "Charleston," answer the following questions by filling in the blanks.

1. <u>Vulnerable</u> means _____.

2. What is the name of the famous military college in Charleston?

3. What was the original name of Charleston?

4. What is Charleston's average annual temperature?

5. What is the name of Charleston's famous festival?

6. What was the name of the hurricane that struck the city in 1989?

Remember, if you don't know what a word means, look it up in a dictionary! You'll do better in the exercises!

7. Which vocabulary word means <u>to give variety to</u>?

Total Correct _____

Name

WRITING CHALLENGE

Your mission is to write a story in the space below. Use your imagination; pick something you like or a topic you are interested in to get started. You can write about anything: places you have visited, a friend, your family, a sport you like or something that has happened to you. If you can't think of anything, then use the power of your mind and create or make up a story. This is called fiction writing. Have fun!

Capitalization & Grammar Guide

Use this quick reference chart to answer your grammatical questions

Capitalize:

✔ the first word of every sentence

✔ all proper nouns and proper adjectives

✔ the first word in a direct quotation

✔ the first word in the greeting and the closing of a letter

✔ names of people and also the initials or abbreviations that stand for those names

✔ titles used with names of persons and abbreviations standing for those titles

✔ the first letter of all principal words in a title

✔ names of the days of the week, months of the year, and as special holidays

✔ names of languages, races, nationalities, religions, and proper adjectives formed from them

✔ all principal words in titles of books, periodicals, poems, stories, articles, movies, paintings and other works of art

✔ geographic names and sections of the country or world

✔ names of special events, historical events, government bodies, documents, and periods of time

✔ names of organizations, institutions, associations, teams, and their members

✔ names of businesses and brand names of their products

✔ abbreviations of titles and organizations

✔ words that refer to a specific deity and sacred books

✔ words denoting family relationships, such as mother, father, brother, aunt, uncle, etc., only when these words stand for the name of the same individual

✔ use all caps for acronyms such as FBI, CIA, or NFL

Punctuation Rules:

A period is used...
✔ at the end of a declarative sentence as well as a mild imperative sentence

✔ after initials and abbreviations

✔ at the end of some rhetorical questions

✔ after numbers and letters in outlines

✔ inside quotation marks at the end of the sentence

✔ only once for sentences ending with an abbreviation

✔ as a decimal point and to separate dollars and cents

A semicolon is used...
✔ to separate two independent clauses very close in meaning but not separated by and, but, or, nor, for, or yet

✔ to separate groups of words or phrases which already contain commas

✔ to connect two independent clauses when the second clause begins with a conjunctive adverb. (most of the time it is better to break the sentence into two separate parts)

A colon is used...
✔ sometimes after the greeting of a formal letter

✔ before a list of items or details, especially after expressions like, "as follows" and "the following"

✔ before a long, formal statement or quotation

✔ between independent clauses when the second clause explains the first clause

✔ between the parts of a number which indicate time

Parentheses are used...
✔ to enclose incidental explanatory matter which is added to a sentence but is not considered of major importance

✔ to enclose an author's insertion or comment

GRAMMAR GUIDE
Use this quick reference chart to answer your grammatical questions

A comma is used...
- to separate words, phrases, or clauses in a series (at least three items)
- to set off a direct quotation
- after greetings or salutations in a letter
- after the words "yes" and "no" when they begin a sentence
- to separate the names of a city and state in addresses
- to separate the month and day from the year in a date
- to set off a word, phrase, or clause that interrupts the main thought of a sentence
- to separate a noun of direct address from the rest of the sentence
- to separate two or more adjectives which modify the same noun
- to enclose a title, name, or initials which follow a person's last name
- to separate an appositive or any other explanatory phrase from the rest of the sentence
- to separate two independent clauses in a compound sentence joined by such words as: but, or, for, so, yet
- to separate digits in a number greater than 999 except in street names and addresses.
- to make the meaning clear whenever necessary

A hyphen is used...
- to divide a word at the end of a line (divide only between syllables)
- to join the words in compound numbers from twenty-one to ninety-nine and with fractions used as adjectives
- with the prefixes ex-, self-, all-, with the suffix -elect, and with all prefixes before a proper noun or proper adjective
- to prevent confusion or awkwardness
- to separate compound modifiers, two or more words expressing a single concept, when they precede a noun (for example, know-it-all attitude, or, full-time job)

Dashes are used...
- to indicate an abrupt break in thought in the sentence
- to mean namely, in other words, that is, etc. before an explanation
- to use between numbers in a page reference

A question mark is used...
- at the end of a direct question (an interrogative sentence)
- inside quotation marks when the quotation is a question

An exclamation mark is used...
- after a word, phrase, or sentence that expresses strong feeling
- inside quotation marks when the quotation is an exclamation

Quotation marks are used...
- to set off a direct quotation–a person's exact words (Single quotation marks are used for quotes within quotes)
- to enclose titles of chapters, articles, short stories, poems, songs and other parts of books and periodicals
- to set off slang and foreign words

Underlining, or italics, is used...
- for titles of books, plays, magazines, newspapers, films, ships, radio and TV programs, music albums, works of art
- to emphasize words, letters, and figures referred to as such and for foreign words